A Treasury of Uyghur Proverbs

Bridging Cultures, Keeping Wisdom

Memet T Zunun

Uyghur Language Studies

London 2024

Preface

Proverbs, timeless expressions of wisdom, have been passed down through generations, transcending cultures and eras. These concise sayings capture insights into life, values, and the human experience. Among Turkic-speaking peoples, Uyghur proverbs are some of the earliest, reflecting a deep-rooted tradition of conveying knowledge and moral lessons.

Proverbs, emerging from ancient civilisations, have consistently communicated the essence of their cultures. Throughout history, they have been preserved in religious texts, literature, and collections, revealing the wisdom of societies across time. Their adaptability and continued relevance in modern life highlight their enduring value as a timeless guide to our shared cultural heritage. These concise sayings, enriched with wisdom, offer guidance and understanding that remains as vital today as ever.

My journey with proverbs began in 1990 when I compiled an English-Chinese-Uyghur trilingual dictionary of proverbs. Although this work was not published then, my dedication to it has never wavered. Over the years, I have continually refined and expanded the collection, ensuring its quality constantly improves. Whenever I encountered a proverb related to Uyghur or its English equivalent, I recorded it, contributing to the ongoing evolution and improvement of the collection.

Memet T Zunun

London

Contents

Uyghur Proverb

The Uyghur people, a Turkic ethnic group, primarily reside in a region that has recently garnered significant media attention. This area has different names depending on perspective. Chinese authorities officially call it the Xinjiang Uyghur Autonomous Region, commonly known as Xinjiang. In contrast, many Uyghur diaspora members and activists prefer terms such as Eastern Turkistan, Uyghur Region, or Uyghurstan. Researchers and historians may also use older terms like Sinkiang or Chinese Turkistan, especially in historical contexts.

Uyghur proverbs have a rich history deeply rooted in the Uyghur people's cultural heritage. The earliest recorded instances can be traced back to the time of the Uyghur Khaganate (745–840), a powerful empire that spanned the Mongolian steppes. The Orkhon inscriptions and monuments from this period include some of these early proverbs, which capture the wisdom and insights from the Uyghur people's experiences.

After migrating to the Tarim Basin and surrounding areas in 840 and uniting with local Uyghur populations, the Uyghur people preserved, flourished and cultivated their proverbs, which became integral to their cultural preservation. These proverbs passed down values, traditions, and accumulated knowledge across generations. The significance of Uyghur proverbs is well documented in Mahmud Kashgari's *Compendium of the Turkic Dialects (Dīwān Lughāt al-Turk)*, compiled between 1072 and 1074, which recognised the linguistic and cultural diversity of Turkic peoples, including the Uyghurs.

During the six centuries of the Chagatai Language period (14th–20th century), also known as Turki, Eastern Turkic, or Chagatai Turkic, an influential Turkic language widely spoken across Central Asia, Uyghur proverbs underwent a significant evolution, mirroring the dynamism of Uyghur cultural traditions. These proverbs served as a means of communication, conveying moral lessons, practical advice, and insights into various aspects of life. Throughout this period, Uyghur proverbs were refined and solidified as essential to Uyghur cultural identity.

Today, Uyghur proverbs testify to the Uyghur people's historical legacy, linguistic richness, and cultural depth. They offer a window into the collective wisdom and ethos of the Uyghur community, exemplifying the resilience and enduring spirit of Uyghur culture throughout history.

This collection presents over 600 Uyghur proverbs and their English equivalents, underscoring their significance and vibrant presence within contemporary Uyghur oral traditions. Uyghur people regularly integrate these proverbs into conversations, highlighting their cultural importance and relevance. The proverbs often draw on nature, using vivid animal and nature imagery to capture emotions and convey complex situations. Some have evolved into distinct traditional sayings with deep significance within the Uyghur community, reflecting the blending of beliefs and thoughts tailored to their intricate life circumstances.

The *Compendium of the Turkic Dialects* (Kashgari, 1981), completed in the 11th century by Mahmud Kashgari, is the earliest extensive collection of Uyghur proverbs, with more than 270 entries. Since then, proverbs have continued to evolve and find their place in classical Uyghur literature. This compilation draws from reputable sources such as

Kashgari's work, Rahim's *Uyghur Proverbs* (Rahim, 1979, 1990), and Yaqup's *Explanatory Dictionary of the Uyghur Language* (Yaqup, 1990–1998), ensuring the credibility of the selected proverbs. The selection process involved considering each proverb's cultural significance, linguistic clarity, and potential for cross-cultural understanding. Uyghur proverbs are characterised by clarity, conciseness, straightforwardness, and traditional nature. Due to their popularity and potential for cross-cultural borrowing, certain proverbs may be shared across multiple languages. However, exploring the origins of these proverbs in detail is beyond the scope of this collection.

This collection fosters cross-cultural understanding by including specific Uyghur proverbs alongside their English equivalents. Despite linguistic disparities and the challenges of finding precise counterparts in English, the collection aims to provide meaningful connections between Uyghur and English proverbs. It offers a nuanced understanding of their meanings and a deeper appreciation of the similarities and differences in their connotations.

Owing to their popularity and potential cross-cultural borrowing, it is plausible that some proverbs are shared among multiple languages. While certain Uyghur proverbs may have versions in different languages, this collection only delves into their origins. For instance, one Uyghur proverb bears a striking similarity to its English counterpart:

    Tömürni qiziqida soq.
Strike while the iron is hot.
Idiomatic Meaning: Make hay while the sun shines; strike while the iron is hot

Awareness of the cultural and linguistic context when interpreting proverbs and using specific terms is crucial.

Understanding "adem" as a gender-neutral pronoun in Uyghur proverbs helps ensure inclusivity and avoids potential misinterpretation or exclusion. For example:

Kiyim ademning zinniti, iger atning (zinniti).
Clothes embellish a man, while a saddle adorns a horse.
Idiomatic Meaning: Clothes maketh the man.

Like many other languages and cultures, Uyghur proverbs may have variations or slight modifications while conveying a similar underlying meaning. This characteristic is common among proverbs across different cultures, allowing for creativity and adaptability while preserving the essence and wisdom they carry. It highlights the flexibility of language and the ability to express timeless truths in various ways. These variations in Uyghur proverbs contribute to the richness and diversity of the language and offer insights into the cultural nuances of different regions and communities. For instance:

Adem zinnia kilim, Terex qimmiti gopuram.
Clothes make the man, while leaves define the tree.
Idiomatic Meaning: Clothes maketh the man.

Translating proverbs between languages can be complex, as direct equivalents may not exist due to cultural, linguistic, and contextual differences. It requires a deep understanding of both languages and the ability to capture the proverb's essence and intended meaning while adapting it to the target language.

It is essential to consider that proverbs are deeply rooted in their cultural and historical contexts, and capturing their whole meaning and nuances in another language can be challenging. Translators often strive to find the closest possible equivalent or a phrase that conveys a similar concept or wisdom.

In the case of Uyghur proverbs, where direct equivalents may be scarce, diligent efforts are required to ensure accurate and appropriate translations. It involves delving into the cultural background, studying the nuances of both languages and making informed decisions to present a fitting translation conveying the original proverb's essence. It is a delicate process that necessitates respect for both languages and their unique expressions of wisdom.

For instance:

Xudayim qilar toqquz, men qilarmen ottuz.
God does nine, and I do thirty.
Idiomatic Meaning: Man proposes, God disposes.

Dostung qagha bolsa yëyishing poq.
If your friend is a crow, you feast on filth.
Idiomatic Meaning: If you lie down with dogs, you will get up with fleas; a man is known by the company he keeps.

Bilimdin artuq bayliq yoq.
There is no wealth more remarkable than knowledge.
Literal Meaning: It underscores knowledge's exceptional value and significance compared to material wealth. It suggests that knowledge provides enduring benefits, personal growth, and empowerment, making it a priceless and invaluable asset.

This collection of Uyghur proverbs highlights the enduring role of wisdom in Uyghur society. Proverbs, cherished for their simplicity and wisdom, reflect the transformative power of learning and the profound respect for wisdom in Uyghur culture. Central to this collection is the idea that 'There is no more incredible wealth than knowledge,' underscoring the universal and enduring significance of education and personal growth.

The collection aims to bridge cultural and linguistic gaps by providing English equivalents of Uyghur proverbs, acknowledging that while translations may not fully capture cultural nuances, the core message about the value of knowledge remains clear. Drawing from foundational works like John Heywood's and Jennifer Speake's collections, the goal is to inspire curiosity, promote cross-cultural understanding, and celebrate wisdom's enduring and inspiring role in our lives.

The completion of an English equivalent for Uyghur proverbs would not have been possible without reference to foundational works such as the Proverbs of John Heywood (Heywood, 1874), compiled and published by Tudor courtier John Heywood, and the Oxford Dictionary of Proverbs (Speake, 2008), edited by Jennifer Speake. These invaluable resources ensure a comprehensive exploration of English proverbs and their counterparts.

Due to space constraints in this edition, detailed information such as historical context, earliest datable appearances, and origins of the proverbs are not included, except where referenced in Kashgari's dictionary.

Organisation of Proverbs

This collection of proverbs is organised into two main sections for ease of use and accessibility:

Uyghur to English Section:

Structure: This section presents Uyghur proverbs followed by their English translations. Each entry includes either the idiomatic meaning or if no direct English equivalent exists, a literal translation of its meaning.

Organisation: Proverbs are arranged alphabetically according to the Uyghur Latin script. The Latin script, standardised by the Uyghur Language Committee in 2011, along with the International Phonetic Alphabet (IPA), ensures a consistent and universally understandable representation of the Uyghur language.

English to Uyghur Section:

Structure: This section lists English translations of Uyghur proverbs and provides their Uyghur versions. It follows a straightforward alphabetical sequence, organised by the proverbs' main words, such as "active" in "An active doer surpasses ten mere speakers."

Purpose: This arrangement facilitates easy cross-referencing between English translations and their Uyghurs. proverbs

This organisation enhances navigation and comparison, making it easier to understand and appreciate proverbs in both Uyghur and English.

Comparison of Orthographies

ORDER	UEY	ULY	IPA
1	ئا	a a	/ɑ/
2	ئە	e e	/ɛ/~/æ/
3	ب	b b	/b/
4	پ	p p	/p/
5	ت	t t	/t/
6	ج	j j	/d͡ʒ/
7	چ	ch ch	/t͡ʃ/
8	خ	x x	/χ/
9	د	d d	/d/
10	ر	r r	/r/
11	ز	z z	/z/
12	ژ	zh zh	/ʒ/

13	س	s s	/s/
14	ش	sh sh	/ʃ/
15	غ	gh gh	/ʁ/
16	ف	f f	/f/
17	ق	q q	/q/
18	ك	k k	/k/
19	گ	g g	/g/
20	ڭ	ng ng	/ŋ/
21	ل	l l	/l/
22	م	m m	/m/
23	ن	n n	/n/
24	ھ	h h	/h/
25	ئو	o o	/o/
26	ئۇ	u u	/u/
27	ئۆ	ö ö	/ø/

28	ئۇ	ü ü	/y/
29	ۋ	w w	/w/~/v/
30	ئې	ë ë	/e/
31	ئى	i i	/i/~/ɪ/
32	ي	y y	/j/

Note:

UEY	Uyghur Arabic Script
ULY	Uyghur Latin Script
IPA	International Phonetic Association

References

1. **Heywood, J.** (1874). *The Proverbs of John Heywood: Being the "proverbs" of that Author printed 1546*. Edited, with notes and introduction by Julian Sharman. London: George Bell and Sons.
2. **Kashgari, M.** (1981). *Turkiy Tillar Diwani (Compendium of the Turkic Dialects)*. Urumchi: Shinjiang Xelq Neshiriyati.
3. **Rahim, M.** (1990). *Uyghur Maqal Temsilliri (Uyghur Proverbs)*. Urumchi: Xinjiang People's Publishing House.
4. **Simpson, J. A.** (1982). *The Concise Oxford Dictionary of Proverbs*. Oxford: Oxford University Press.
5. **Speake, J.** (ed.) (n.d.). *The Oxford Dictionary of Proverbs*. Fifth Edition. Oxford: Oxford University Press.
6. **Yaqup, A.** (1998-1990). *Uyghur Tilining Izahliq Lughiti (Explanatory Dictionary of the Uyghur Language)*. Six Volumes. Urumchi: Xinjiang People's Publishing House.

Uyghur -English

Abdal tallimas.
> A beggar does not choose.
> **Idiomatic Meaning:** beggars can't be choosers.

Ach nëme yëmes, toq nëme dëmes.
> The hungry do not choose when to eat, and the full do not choose when to speak. (Kashgari 1072–74)
> **Idiomatic Meaning:** Out of the fullness of the heart, the mouth speaks.

Achchiq eqilni këser.
> Anger drives the wits away.
> **Literal Meaning:** This proverb warns about the harmful effects of rage on cognitive performance. Allowing anger to take control might impair one's capacity to think clearly, appraise situations objectively, and behave rationally. It emphasises the significance of properly regulating anger and finding constructive ways to address and express it rather than allowing it to dominate reason and rationality.

Achliqni yastuq kötürer.
> Pillow supports hunger.
> **Literal Meaning: It** suggests that when a person is hungry, they can alleviate or temporarily forget their hunger by going to bed and falling asleep. Sleeping can provide temporary relief from the discomfort of hunger, as the person becomes unaware of their hunger while asleep.

Adem adem bilen adem bolar.
> Through the aid of fellow men, a man truly becomes.
> **Idiomatic Meaning:** no man is an island.

Adem balisi eyipsiz bolmas.
> A human child is not flawless. (Kashgari 1072–74)
> **Idiomatic Meaning:** to err is human, to forgive divine.

Adem balisi yoqilar, yaxshi ëti menggülük qalar.
Human children may pass away, yet their noble name
endures for eternity. (Kashgari 1072–74)
Idiomatic Meaning: A good name is better than riches; a
man is not dead while his name is still spoken.

Adem köp yerde ishek haram boptu.
Many people spoil the donkey.
Idiomatic Meaning: Too many cooks spoil the broth;
councils of war never fight.

Adem suni meynet qilar, su ademni pakiz (qilar)
Man pollutes the water, while water purifies the man.
Literal Meaning: It highlights the interconnected
relationship between humans and the environment,
particularly emphasising the impact of human actions on
water resources. It suggests that while humans may
contribute to water pollution, water itself has the potential
to purify or cleanse individuals. It emphasises the
importance of recognising the impact of human actions on
the environment, specifically water resources, and the
potential for water to offer restorative properties. It
encourages responsible behaviours and a deeper
appreciation for water's vital role in sustaining life.

Adem zinniti kiyim, derex qimmiti yopurmaq.
Clothes make the man, while leaves define the tree.
Idiomatic Meaning: Clothes maketh the man.

Ademning alisi ichide, haywanning alisi tëshida.
Animal colours show; man's true colours hide. (Kashgari
1072–74)
Literal Meaning: It highlights a perceived contrast
between the visibility of animals' physical characteristics
and the concealed nature of human attributes or qualities.
It suggests that humans can hide or conceal their true
colours or inner selves, making it more challenging to
discern their true intentions or character.

Aghzida külke - chaqchaq, qoynida palta – pichaq.
Despite the concealed axe in the heart, laughter lingers
upon the lips.
Literal Meaning: It suggests that even though someone
may appear smiling or cheerful on the surface, their true
intentions or emotions may differ. It implies that there
may be hidden pain, sadness, or negative feelings despite
the outward display of happiness. This proverb reminds us
that people's true feelings and intentions are not always
evident from their external demeanour. It highlights that
someone may be masking their emotions behind a facade
of humour or light-heartedness.

Aghzinggha qan bolsimu, düshminingning aldida tükürme.
Hold your spit before foes, even with blood in your
mouth.
Literal Meaning: It advises against displaying weakness
or vulnerability in the presence of adversaries or those
who may wish you harm. It suggests maintaining a
dignified demeanour, even in challenging circumstances.

Akang kimni alsa yenggeng shu.
Whomever your brother weds becomes your sister-in-law.
Literal Meaning: It implies accepting and adapting to
the outcomes and circumstances arising from a particular
situation. It signifies a recognition that life's events and
relationships are not always within our control, and it
encourages individuals to embrace the path that unfolds,
even if it may bring unexpected or challenging situations.

Ala inekning balisi, chala quyruq.
The calf of a black pied cattle bears a short tail.
Idiomatic Meaning: Like mother, like daughter; Like
father, like son.

Aldimgha keldi dep yëme, aghzimgha keldi dep dëme.
Do not consume whatever comes your way, nor speak
whatever your mind may say.

Literal Meaning: It encourages us to be intentional in our actions and mindful of the impact our decisions and words may have on ourselves and others. It promotes making conscious choices and practising thoughtful communication, leading to better outcomes and healthier relationships.

Aldirap ghora yëmeng, pütün chiqar.
Patience is required with the green apricot, or it shall pass undigested as a whole.
Idiomatic Meaning: Nothing should be done in haste but gripping a flea.

Aldiraqsan chiwin sütke chüsher.
Fly in haste falls into the milk. (Kashgari 1072–74)
Idiomatic Meaning: hasty climbers have sudden falls.

Aldirighan nede këtip baridu, aldirimighanning keynide.
Where the busy one ventures, trails the one unhurried.
Idiomatic Meaning: More haste, less speed.

Aldirighan putlishar.
Haste stumbles.
Idiomatic Meaning: Nothing should be done in haste but gripping a flea.

Aldirighan yolda qalar.
A hasty person often finds themselves stuck along the road.
Idiomatic Meaning: hasty climbers have sudden falls.

Aldirighanda ëshiki yëtiwaptu.
When in a hurry, the donkey chooses to lie down.
Literal Meaning: It emphasises the frustrating nature of encountering obstacles or delays when in a hurry, comparing it to a donkey unexpectedly laying down and hindering progress. It reminds us to remain patient, adaptable, and prepared for unexpected challenges, even when efficiency and speed are essential.

Aldirighanda ishtanbagh ikki chigilip qaptu.
In his haste, his pants tangled twice.
Idiomatic Meaning: more haste, less speed; nothing should be done in haste but gripping a flea.

Aldirighanning ishi chala.
The hasty man's work remains undone.
Idiomatic Meaning: nothing should be done in haste but gripping a flea.

Alemning köz - quliqi bar.
The universe possesses eyes and ears.
Idiomatic Meaning: fields have eyes, and woods have ears.

Alla dëgen bendisige, ekilip bërer mehellisige.
If it is God's will for a man to possess, he shall deliver it to his door.
Idiomatic Meaning: if God had wanted man to fly, he would have given him wings.

Almaqning bermiki bar, barmaqning kelmiki (bar)
You must give when you take and return when you go.
Idiomatic Meaning: Give the devil his due; give and take is fair play.

Alp septe sinilar, dana yighinda.
The hero is tested within the team; the wise man is tested within the counsel. (Kashgari 1072–74)
Literal Meaning: It highlights that heroes are tested in team settings, where their leadership and ability to work collaboratively are evaluated. On the other hand, wise individuals are tested within counsel settings, where their knowledge and ability to provide insightful guidance are examined. This proverb emphasises the importance of recognizing and valuing different qualities and tests individuals may face based on their roles and strengths.

Altun chirimas.
Gold does not get rusted.
Idiomatic Meaning: If gold rusts what can iron do.

Aqar su purimaydu.
Flowing water does not stink.
Literal Meaning: It conveys the idea that water in motion tends to stay fresh and free from unpleasant odours. Metaphorically, it encourages individuals to embrace movement, change, and progress to avoid stagnation and undesirable outcomes in various aspects of life.

Arghamcha ajiz yëridin üzülidu.
The rope breaks at its weak link.
Idiomatic Meaning: a chain is no stronger than its weakest link.

Arman'gha chushluq derman yoq.
The spirit is will, but power is weak.
Idiomatic Meaning: The spirit is willing, but the flesh is weak.

Arpisiz at qir ashalmas, yademchisiz alp sepni yimirelmes.
Just as a horse cannot run without oats, a hero cannot fight without support (Kashgari 1072–74)
Idiomatic Meaning: an army marches on its stomach.

Arslan hörkirse, at ayighi kalwalishidu.
When a lion roars, a horse's hooves tremble in fear. (Kashgari 1072–74)
Literal Meaning: It symbolises the ability of a dominant and powerful force to evoke fear or unease in those who are comparatively weaker or more vulnerable. It highlights the impact of a commanding presence and metaphorically underscores the contrast between strength and vulnerability.

Arslan qërisa, chashqanning uwasini köziter.
> When the lion is old, guard the mouse's nest. (Kashgari 1072–74)
> **Literal Meaning: It** underscores the ageing lion's scarcity of prey options and its necessity to patiently wait for even a mouse to satisfy its hunger. Metaphorically, it speaks to the challenges of ageing and the need to adapt and make the best of the available circumstances.

Artuq gep, ëshekke yük.
> Excessive talk burdens the donkey's load.
> **Idiomatic Meaning:** Brag is a good dog, but holdfast is better.

Ash bergen qazanni chaqma.
> Do not break the pot that feeds you.
> **Idiomatic Meaning:** Don't bite the hand that feeds you.

At alsang ay këngesh, xotun alsang yil (këngesh)
> If you buy a horse, seek advice for a month; if you marry, seek advice for a year.
> **Idiomatic Meaning:** Never choose your women or your linen by candlelight.

At atangche bolsimu at, yerge qozuq qëqip baghlap yat.
> Even if your horse is like your father, tie it up before you rest.
> **Idiomatic Meaning:** Trust in God but tie your camel.

At aylinip oqurni tapar, qoy aylinip qotanni (tapar)
> A horse roams and finds its stable, while a sheep circles the sheepfold.
> **Idiomatic Meaning:** The apple never falls far from the tree.

Ata balisi atisidek tughular.
> A child shall be born resembling his father. (Kashgari 1072–74)

Idiomatic Meaning: Like father, like son, the apple never falls far from the tree.

Atalmas oqidin, chichalmas poqidin körer.
One who cannot shoot blames the bullet, and one who cannot defecate blames the faeces.
Idiomatic Meaning: A bad workman blames his tools.

Atqan oq yёnip kelmes, ötken waqIt qaytip (kelmes)
A shot will not return; the past cannot be called back.
Idiomatic Meaning: Things past cannot be recalled.

Atqan oqni yandurghili bolmas, chiqqan sözni qayturghili (bolmas)
Once a shot is fired and words are spoken, they cannot be withdrawn.
Idiomatic Meaning: What's done cannot be undone; a word spoken is past recalling.

Awwal oyla, andin sözle.
Think first, then speak.
Idiomatic Meaning: think first and speak afterwards; think before you speak.

Ay tolun bolsa, qol bilen imlenmes.
The full moon needs no hand to be revealed.
Idiomatic Meaning: The point is plain as a pike staff.

Ayning onbeshi ayding, onbeshi qarangghu.
Half a month shines bright, while the other half resides in darkness.
Literal Meaning: It reflects the natural cycle of the lunar month, with the moon going through phases of brightness and darkness. Metaphorically, it symbolises the fluctuating nature of life and serves as a reminder of the transient and changing aspects of our experiences.

Ayrilghanni ёyiq yeptu, bölün'genni böre (yeptu)/ ayrilghanni ёyiq yer, bölün'genni böri (yer)

The bear devours the lone one; the separated one falls to
the wolf.
Idiomatic Meaning: A house divided cannot stand.

Az bolsimu köpke tawap qil.
Embrace it, even if it is meagre.
Idiomatic Meaning: Every little helps.

Az bolsun, saz bolsun.
Let it be little, but the best.
Literal Meaning: It advises valuing quality over
quantity, suggesting that something of a smaller scale or
extent can be more valuable and impactful if it is of the
highest calibre. It promotes a mindset that values
excellence, simplicity, and focusing on what truly matters.

Bagda gül bolmisa, bulbul kelip sayramas.
When the garden lacks flowers, the nightingale's song
fades away.
Literal Meaning: This proverb can be interpreted to
suggest that to experience or achieve something positive
or delightful, certain foundational elements or
circumstances must be in place. It serves as a reminder
that certain factors must align for a desired outcome. The
proverb can also be seen as a poetic expression
highlighting the interdependence and interconnectedness
of nature, where the presence of flowers in the garden
plays a role in attracting the nightingale's song.

Baghlaqtiki It - owgha yarimaptu.
A dog that is tied is not fit for hunting.
Idiomatic Meaning: A cat in gloves catches no mice.

Bala kelse qoshlap këler, bir - birini bashlap (këler)
When disaster arrives, it often comes in pairs, each
leading the other.
Idiomatic Meaning: bad things come in threes;
misfortunes never come singly.

Bala qaza körünüp kelmes, put - qolini sanggilitip.
Misfortunes never come noticed.
Idiomatic Meaning: Misfortunes never come on their own.

Baliliq öy bazar; balisiz öy mazar.
A house with children is a bustling market; a house without children is a quiet graveyard.
Literal Meaning: It highlights the contrasting atmospheres created by the presence or absence of children in a home. It emphasises the liveliness, energy, and cheerfulness children bring to a household and the potential sense of emptiness or sadness in a home without them.

Balini yashtin öget.
Teach while the child is young.
Idiomatic Meaning: Bend the willow while it is young.

Belge bolsa yoldin azmas, bilim bolsa sözdin qaymas.
When there is a sign, you are not lost; with knowledge, you are not lost for words. (Kashgari 1072–74)
Literal Meaning: It emphasises the value of guidance and knowledge in different contexts. It suggests that having a sign or guidance prevents one from getting lost physically or metaphorically, while knowledge enables effective communication and expression.

Bëliqning özi suda, közi tashqirida.
The fish resides in the water yet keeps its eyes beyond. (Kashgari 1072–74)
Literal Meaning: It emphasises the unique adaptation of a fish's anatomy, where its eyes remain outside the water despite residing within it. Metaphorically, it highlights the importance of maintaining awareness, adaptability, and an external perspective even when fully engaged in a specific context or activity.

Bergen qol, alghan qoldin yaxshi.
> A hand given is better than a hand received.
> **Idiomatic Meaning: It** is better to give than to receive.

Berginige shükür qil.
> Thanks for the giving.
> **Idiomatic Meaning:** When all fruit fails, welcome haws.

Besh barmaq tekshi emes.
> Five fingers are uneven. (Kashgari 1072–74)
> **Literal Meaning: It** draws a parallel between the unevenness of fingers and the diverse nature of life's circumstances. It suggests that situations and experiences vary from person to person, and it is essential to acknowledge and respond to the uniqueness of each circumstance.

Besh qolni bir yoli aghzigha tiqqili bolmas.
> Do not have five fingers in your mouth.
> **Idiomatic Meaning:** Don't have too many irons in the fire.

Bëshingni salqin, putungni issiq tut, tenning saqliqi, janning rahiti.
> Cool the head and warm the feet for a healthy body and a soul retreat.
> **Idiomatic Meaning:** The head and feet keep warm, the rest will take no harm.

Bextsiz quduqqa chüshse, qum yaghar.
> Even the sand will follow if an unlucky person falls into a well. (Kashgari 1072–74)
> **Literal Meaning: It** conveys that unfortunate individuals in difficult situations may encounter additional misfortunes or challenges. It serves as a reminder of the potential for a series of unfortunate events to unfold when someone is already experiencing bad luck.

Bikar yürme laghaylap, pulni xejle awaylap.
Do not spend your time idly, and spend your money wisely.
Idiomatic Meaning: what you spend, you have.

Bikargha tamaq berse, tuzi kem deptu.
One who receives free food complains about the absence of salt.
Idiomatic Meaning: Don't look a gift horse in the mouth.

Bilim alay dëseng, özüngning bilimsiz ikenlikini iqrar qil.
To acquire knowledge, acknowledge your ignorance.
Literal Meaning: It emphasises the importance of humility and a willingness to acknowledge one's lack of knowledge. It suggests that authentic learning and growth occur when individuals approach new information or experiences with an open mind and genuinely recognise their ignorance. By embracing a humble attitude, individuals create space for new knowledge and understanding to enter their lives.

Bilim ëlish altun yighishtinmu artuq.
Acquiring knowledge is worth more than amassing gold.
Literal Meaning: It underscores knowledge's immense value and significance compared to material possessions. It suggests that acquiring and cultivating knowledge brings more significant benefits and personal development than accumulating wealth alone.

Bilim ëlish yingnide quduq kolighandek.
Learning is akin to drilling a hole with a needle.
Literal Meaning: It underscores the challenging and meticulous nature of the learning process. It emphasises that acquiring knowledge or mastering a new skill often involves patience, precision, and focused effort.

Bilim eqilning chirighi.
Knowledge is the light of the mind.
Literal Meaning: It highlights the illuminating and

transformative nature of knowledge. It suggests that knowledge brings clarity, understanding, and expansion of consciousness, allowing individuals to navigate the complexities of life and make informed decisions.

Bilim küch.

Knowledge is power.
Idiomatic Meaning: Knowledge is power.

Bilimdin artuq bayliq yoq.

There is no wealth more remarkable than knowledge.
Literal Meaning: It underscores knowledge's exceptional value and significance compared to material wealth. It suggests that knowledge provides enduring benefits, personal growth, and empowerment, making it a priceless and invaluable asset in one's life.

Bilimi azning achchiqi yaman.

The wrath of the ignorant is a formidable force.
Literal Meaning: It cautions against anger's destructive potential when coupled with a lack of knowledge or understanding. It emphasises the importance of cultivating awareness, knowledge, and empathy to avoid or address anger more objectively and constructively.

Bilimi küchlük mingni yënger, biliki küchlük birni.

A knowledgeable mind conquers a thousand with wisdom, whereas a strong hand defeats only one with strength.
Literal Meaning: It underscores the superiority of knowledge and intellectual capacity over physical strength. It emphasises the importance of intelligence, strategic thinking, and informed decision-making when confronting challenges or adversaries. It suggests these attributes can lead to successful outcomes even in unfavourable circumstances.

Bilimlik adem - yëqimliq adem.

A knowledgeable man is a pleasant man.

Literal Meaning: It indicates that individuals with knowledge and understanding often exhibit positive qualities that make them pleasant to interact with. Their ability to contribute insights, engage in meaningful conversations, and provide intellectual stimulation can enhance the overall enjoyment of engaging with them.

Bilimlik adem alim, bilimsiz adem zalim.
A knowledgeable person becomes a scholar; an ignorant person becomes a tyrant.
Literal Meaning: It highlights the positive attributes of knowledge and ignorance's negative consequences. It suggests that knowledge enables individuals to become scholars, contributing to the betterment of society, while ignorance may lead to tyrannical behaviour and negative impacts on others.

Bilimlik özini eyibler, bilimsiz dostini.
The wise blame themselves; the ignorant blame friends.
Literal Meaning: It highlights the contrasting behaviours of individuals with knowledge and those without. It suggests that learned individuals exhibit self-reflection and personal accountability, while the ignorant may blame others rather than examine their actions.

Bilimlikke hörmet qil.
Respect the learned.
Literal Meaning: It underscores the importance of valuing and honouring individuals who have acquired knowledge and expertise. It promotes a culture of appreciation for intellectual pursuits, recognising the contributions and wisdom learned individuals bring to society.

Bilimlikning gëpi roshen.
Words of the learned are clear.
Idiomatic Meaning: Who knows most speaks least.

Bilimlikning tedbiri köp.
A wise man has many measures.
Literal Meaning: It emphasises that wisdom involves having a range of approaches, strategies, and perspectives at one's disposal. It signifies the versatility and adaptability of a wise person to navigate various situations and make well-informed decisions.

Bilimsiz adem - mëwisiz derex.
A man without knowledge is like a barren tree bearing no fruit.
Literal Meaning: It emphasises the value of knowledge in an individual's life. It implies that without knowledge, one may struggle to achieve personal growth, productivity, and fulfilment, much like a tree that fails to bear fruit. It underscores the importance of continuous learning, intellectual development, and knowledge acquisition for personal and professional success.

Bilimsiz bash, gewdige yük.
Without knowledge, the head becomes a burden to the body.
Literal Meaning: It emphasises the value of knowledge in utilising one's intellectual capacities. It suggests that without knowledge, an individual's intellectual abilities can become a burden rather than a source of empowerment, hindering personal growth and decision-making. It underscores the significance of continuous learning and acquiring knowledge to maximise cognitive abilities.

Bilimsizge hal ëytquche ichingde sësitiwet.
It is preferable to endure solitude than to seek empathy from the ignorant.
Literal Meaning: It conveys that it may be more beneficial to face internal struggles alone rather than seeking empathy from individuals who lack knowledge or understanding. It underscores the significance of seeking

support from those who can provide meaningful
understanding and empathy.

Bilimsizge pushayman hemrah.
An apology is always a companion to the ignorant.
Literal Meaning: It highlights the tendency of
individuals lacking knowledge or understanding to
apologise for their words or actions. It suggests that
unawareness or lack of knowledge can lead to unintended
harm or mistakes, necessitating the need for apologies to
acknowledge and make amends for such situations.

Bilimsizlik namratliqtin yaman.
Ignorance is worse than poverty.
Idiomatic Meaning: Ignorance is worse than poverty.

Bilmeslik eyib emes, sorimasliq eyib.
Not knowing is not a shame; the shame is not asking.
Idiomatic Meaning: the only stupid question is the one
that is not asked.

Bilmigenni bilimen dep kayima.
Do not pretend to know that which you do not know.
Idiomatic Meaning: let the cobbler stick to his last.

Bilmigenni qilma, bilginingni ayima.
Don't do what you don't know; share what you know.
Idiomatic Meaning: let the cobbler stick to his last.

Bir ana on balini baqar, on bala bir anini baqalmas.
A mother nourishes ten children, yet ten children cannot
care for a mother.
Literal Meaning: It emphasises the unbalanced nature of
a mother's care and the limitations of reciprocal support
from the children. It recognises the immense sacrifice and
selflessness of a mother's love while acknowledging that
the children may not have the same capacity to care for
their mother in the same way.

Bir derwishning bëshi aghrisa, hemme derwishning bëshi aghrimas.
If one dervish has a headache, it does not imply that all dervishes do. (Kashgari 1072–74)
Literal Meaning: It underscores the uniqueness and individuality of people within a group. It cautions against making assumptions or generalisations about an entire group based on the experiences or conditions of one individual, highlighting the importance of recognising and respecting individual differences within a collective.

Bir gül bilen bahar bolmas.
One flower does not make a spring.
Idiomatic Meaning: One swallow does not make a summer.

Bir harghandin, bir achqandin gep sorima.
Do not ask questions of a tired person or a hungry man.
Idiomatic Meaning: The belly has no ears.

Bir kün baldur tërisang, on kün baldur yighisen.
If you sow one day early, you will reap ten days ahead.
Idiomatic Meaning: The sooner begun, the sooner done.

Bir kün yashash üchün, ming kün ögen.
To live a day, one must learn for a thousand days.
Idiomatic Meaning: Live and learn.

Bir qagha bilen qish kelmes.
One crow does not make a winter. (Kashgari 1072–74)
Idiomatic Meaning: One swallow does not make a summer.

Bir qulaqtin kirip bir qulaqtin chiqiptu.
It went in one ear and out the other.
Idiomatic Meaning: in one ear and out the other.

Bir sësiq amut mingni buzar.
One rotten pear can spoil a thousand.

Idiomatic Meaning: The rotten apple injures its neighbour; one rotten apple will spoil the whole barrel; one scabbed sheep mars the whole flock.

Birdin ikki yaxshi, quruq geptin jigde (yaxshi)

Two is better than one, and an oleaster is better than empty promises.
Idiomatic Meaning: Half a loaf is better than no bread; fifty percent of something is better than one hundred percent of nothing; something is better than nothing.

Birinchi küni mëhman, ikkinchi küni xiyman. Üchinchi küni mayaq, tötinchi küni tayaq.

On the first day, he's a guest; on the second, a visitor. By the third day, he's a burden; by the fourth, a stick is needed to drive him away.
Idiomatic Meaning: Fish and guests stink after three days.

Birning eqli bir bolidu, köpning eqli köp (bolidu)

One person has one mind; many people have many minds.
Idiomatic Meaning: When spider webs unite, they can tie up a lion; Many hands make light work.

Biteley oghriliqqa chiqsa ayding boptu.

When the unlucky one steals, the full moon shows up.
Literal Meaning: It implies a belief that when an already unlucky person engages in theft, it aligns with the occurrence of a full moon. It suggests a connection between the individual's misfortune and the timing of this symbolic event, emphasising the interplay between personal circumstances and supernatural or symbolic occurrences.

Biteley quduqqa kirse, shamal ëlip chiqar.

If an unlucky man enters the well, the wind will blow him out. (Kashgari 1072–74)
Literal Meaning: It suggests that an already unlucky individual in a difficult situation may face additional

challenges or setbacks from the wind. The wind
symbolises the amplification of misfortune and the
potential for external factors to worsen their
circumstances further.

Boghuzlaymen dёseng, qoymu tipirlaydu .
> If you slaughter, even the sheep will tremble.
> **Idiomatic Meaning:** Tread on a worm and it will turn.

Bolsang yalghuz seperlik, bolur ishing xeterlik.
> If you travel alone, your journey may be difficult.
> **Idiomatic Meaning:** he travels dangerously who travels
> alone.

Bӧre qoshnisini yёmes.
> Wolf does not devour its neighbours. (Kashgari 1072–74)
> **Idiomatic Meaning:** hawks will not pick out hawks'
> eyes.

Bӧre uwisigha qarap huwlisa qotur bolur.
> It is an ill wolf that howls at its own den.
> **Idiomatic Meaning:** It's an ill bird that fouls its own
> nest.

Bӧridin qorqqan qoy baqmas.
> One who fears the wolf can tend to the sheep.
> **Idiomatic Meaning:** If you can't stand the heat, get out
> of the kitchen.

Bӧrini qotangha bashlima.
> Do not lead a wolf to the sheepfold.
> **Idiomatic Meaning:** Do not call a wolf to help you
> against the dogs.

Bosh taghar ӧre turmas.
> An empty sack does not stand upright.
> **Literal Meaning: It** emphasises the significance of
> substance, value, or knowledge in achieving success or
> influence. It highlights the idea that something or

someone lacking content or worth is unlikely to be stable, respected, or successful.

Bosh yaghachni qurt yeydu.
Worms cling to a soft tree.
Literal Meaning: It suggests that opportunistic individuals target and exploit the vulnerabilities of those who are weak or easily influenced. It underscores the importance of being aware and cautious of individuals seeking to exploit our weaknesses or manipulate us for their benefit.

Bughday nëning bolmisa, bughday sözüng yoqmidi?.
Don't you have a kind word, even if you don't have wheat bread?.
Idiomatic Meaning: say something nice or say nothing at all.

Bughdayning bahaniside, qarimuq su ichiptu.
Because of wheat, the cowherb waters itself. (Kashgari 1072–74)
Idiomatic Meaning: a rising tide lifts all boats.

Bügünki ishni etige qoyma.
Do not leave today's work for tomorrow.
Idiomatic Meaning: Never put off till tomorrow what you can do today.

Bük-baraqsan sögetke qush qonar, chirayliq qizgha söz këler.
A bird will land on a branchy willow, and suitors will come to a beautiful girl. (Kashgari 1072–74)
Literal Meaning: It suggests that beauty can attract attention and result in various expectations or demands placed on an individual. It highlights the complex relationship between attractiveness and the interactions or responsibilities that may arise from it.

Bumu ötüp këtidu.
This, too, shall pass.
Idiomatic Meaning: This, too, shall pass.

Buzmaq asan, qurmaq tes.
It is easier to destroy than to build.
Idiomatic Meaning: Glass, china, and reputation are easily cracked and never well mended.

Chala molla[1] walaqlaydu, egiri noghuch taraqlaydu.
An illiterate mullah speaks loudly; a crooked rolling pin makes noise.
Idiomatic Meaning: A little knowledge is a dangerous thing; empty vessels make the most sound; it's the empty can that makes the most noise.

Chapan qanche kona bolsimu yamghurgha yarar.
No matter how old the jacket is, it's still good for rain. (Kashgari 1072–74)
Literal Meaning: It highlights the enduring functionality and value of something, regardless of its age or appearance, specifically in the context of protection against rain. It serves as a reminder to recognise objects' intrinsic worth and practicality, even if they may not hold the same value in other aspects.

Chapiqini alimen dep qarighu qiptu.
To remove the eye's dirt, one makes a man blind.
Idiomatic Meaning: When you are in a hole, stop digging.

Chaqmaq chüshse ot tutishar, söz anglitilsa meqset biliner.
When lightning strikes, it ignites; when words are explained, the purpose is known. (Kashgari 1072–74)
Literal Meaning: It emphasises the importance of clarity and explanation in fostering understanding and revealing the intended meaning or purpose behind someone's words

---

[1] Mullah

or actions. It suggests that just as lightning leads to fire, explanations lead to comprehension and unveiling of intentions.

Chawa yagh su yëghining ornini basalmas.
Omentum is not a substitute for cooking oil. (Kashgari 1072–74)
Literal Meaning: This proverb highlights the importance of using the appropriate resources and tools for a particular task. Omentum, a fatty tissue membrane in the abdominal cavity of animals, is unsuitable for cooking oil use. It conveys that substituting an inadequate or incompatible material or resource for a required one is unlikely to yield the desired results. The proverb serves as a metaphor, urging individuals to recognise the value of using the right ingredients, tools, or methods for a given situation. It suggests that taking shortcuts or using inappropriate substitutes can lead to subpar outcomes or even failure. In a broader sense, the proverb encourages thoroughness, preparedness, and adherence to proper practices in various aspects of life. It advises against cutting corners, compromising quality, or replacing essential elements with inadequate alternatives.

Chawangni chitqa yayma.
Keep your negativity confined within.
Idiomatic Meaning: Don't wash your dirty linen in public.

Chiqmighan janda ümid bar.
While not dead, hope forever persists.
Idiomatic Meaning: Where there is a will, there is a way.

Chiqqan sözni qayturghili (bolmas)
Once spoken, words cannot be undone.
Idiomatic Meaning: what's done cannot be undone.

Chirayigha nan chilap ichkili bolmaydu.
Beauty is not nourished by sipping tea.
Idiomatic Meaning: Appearances can be deceptive.

Chirayliq chirayliq emes, köygen chirayliq.
Beautiful is not beautiful; love is beautiful.
Idiomatic Meaning: Beauty is in the eye of the beholder.

Chirayliq söz tashni yumshitar.
A kind word can soften even the hardest stone.
Idiomatic Meaning: discretion is the better part of valour.

Chirayliq yüzde emes, sözde.
Beauty is not in a face, but in words (actions)
Idiomatic Meaning: beauty is only skin-deep.

Chong bëliq kichik bëliqni yeptu.
Big fish eats the little fish.
Idiomatic Meaning: big fish eat little fish.

Chong nan pishqiche, kichik toqach köyüp boptu.
Before the large loaf was baked, the small loaf was charred.
Idiomatic Meaning: a little pot is soon hot.

Chongning achchiqi kelgüche, kichikning jëni chiqiptu.
Before an elder's anger ignites, young souls blaze with fury.
Idiomatic Meaning: a little pot is soon hot.

Chongqur östeng asta aqidu.
Deep streams run still.
Idiomatic Meaning: deep waters run still.

Chüje xoraz bilginini chillaydu.
Chicks chirp what they know.
Idiomatic Meaning: shoemaker, not above the sandal.

Chüjini küzde sanang, chöchürini pishqanda (sanang)
Count the chicken in the fall, (count) the ravioli when
cooked.
Idiomatic Meaning: Don't count your chickens before
they hatch.

Chüsh tetürige mangidu.
Dreams go by contraries.
Idiomatic Meaning: Dreams go by contraries.

Derextin mëwe alay dëseng yiltizini asra.
To savour the fruit's sweetness, tend to the roots with
care.
Literal Meaning: It advises individuals to enjoy the
results but also take responsibility for and care for the
foundational aspects supporting them. It promotes a
holistic perspective and reminds us to appreciate and
nurture the underlying factors contributing to our
achievements or desired outcomes.

Doramchining aghzi puchuq.
Imitators have a crooked mouth.
Idiomatic Meaning: Imitation is the sincerest form of
flattery.

Dost keyningde maxtar, düshmen aldingda (maxtar)
A friend praises you behind your back; an enemy only
praises you in front of you.
Literal Meaning: The proverb highlights the contrasting
behaviours of a genuine friend and an insincere enemy. It
reminds us to value and recognise true friends' genuine
praise and support while being cautious about the
intentions behind flattering remarks from those with
ulterior motives. It encourages discernment in identifying
authentic relationships and highlights the importance of
trust and sincerity in friendships.

Dost sözini tashlima, tashlap beshingni qashlima.
Do not disregard a friend's words; if you do, do not be

surprised by the consequences.
Literal Meaning: You should listen to and consider a friend's advice or warnings. If you choose to ignore their counsel, you should be prepared for any adverse outcomes that may result. This advice underscores the importance of trust in a friendship, reassuring you that your friend's guidance is given with your best interests at heart.

Dostning dostluqi bashqa kün chüshkende biliner.
A friend's true friendship shines when you are in need.
Idiomatic Meaning: A friend in need is a friend indeed.

Dostung qagha bolsa yëyishing poq.
If your friend is a crow, you feast on filth.
Idiomatic Meaning: If you lie down with dogs, you will get up with fleas; a man is known by the company he keeps,.

Dozaqning ishikini para achidu.
Bribery opens the gates of hell. (Kashgari 1072–74)
Literal Meaning: It underscores the potential for money to be used as a bribe to exert undue influence and achieve favourable outcomes. **Note**: However, it should be recognised that bribery is illegal, unethical, and harmful to the integrity of institutions and society.

Dunyani su bassa, ördekke nëme ghem.
Even amidst a flooded world, why should the duck be concerned?.
Literal Meaning: It highlights a potential downside of solely focusing on individual needs without considering the well-being of others. It encourages us to reflect on the balance between self-preservation and compassion for others, recognising that empathy and care for our fellow beings are essential to our humanity.

Düshmen siringni oghrilaydu, dost xatayingni toghrilaydu.
An enemy steals your secrets; a friend corrects your errors.

Literal Meaning: The proverb highlights the contrasting actions and intentions of an enemy and a true friend. It serves as a reminder to value and appreciate the role of a true friend in our lives. It highlights the importance of trust, support, and constructive criticism that friends provide while cautioning against the potential harm that enemies can inflict. It emphasises the positive impact of friendship and encourages us to surround ourselves with genuine, caring individuals with our best interests at heart.

Düshmenni sel chaghlisa, bashqa chiqar.
If one disregards the enemy, they risk losing their head. *(Kashgari 1072–74)*
Literal Meaning: It stresses recognising and addressing one's enemies or potential threats. It emphasises the need for vigilance, preparedness, and proactive measures to mitigate risks and protect oneself from harm or negative consequences.

Düshminingning düshmini sëning dostung.
The enemy of your enemy is your friend.
Idiomatic Meaning: The enemy of my enemy is my friend,.

Edeb - exlaq bazarda sëtilmas, edebsizge hëch kishi qëtilmas.
Morality cannot be purchased in the market, and the immoral find themselves isolated.
Literal Meaning: It emphasises the intrinsic worth of moral values, the importance of personal integrity, and its impact on forming meaningful relationships. It serves as a reminder that ethical conduct is essential for building trust and earning the respect and companionship of others.

Edeblik ëghizning sözi güzel.
A polite mouth pours out beautiful words.
Idiomatic Meaning: Handsome is as handsome does; pretty is as pretty does.

Edebni edepsizdin ögen.

Learn manners from the ill-mannered.

Literal Meaning: It encourages us to find lessons in negative examples, particularly regarding etiquette and social behaviour. It promotes self-reflection, appreciation for good manners, and personal growth in our interactions.

Ëghilda oghlaq tughulsa, ëriqta oti üner.

When a lamb is born in a sheep's shed, verdant grass shall line the stream. (Kashgari 1072–74)

Literal Meaning: It symbolises the potential for positive outcomes and growth when favourable circumstances align. It highlights the significance of nurturing environments and the natural progression of abundance and flourishing when conditions are conducive.

Ëghiz saqlighan janni saqlar.

Whoever guards their mouth also saves their own life.

Idiomatic Meaning: A shut mouth catches no flies.

Ëghiz yëse, köz uyilar.

The man who has consumed another's food becomes filled with modesty. (Kashgari 1072–74)

Literal Meaning: It highlights the transformative effect of receiving assistance or hospitality. It underscores the importance of gratitude, a sense of obligation, and humility in acknowledging the support we receive from others. It implies that experiencing the kindness and generosity of others can create a sense of indebtedness or modesty in the recipient.

Ëgilgen bashni qilich kesmeptu.

The bowed head escapes the sword's cut.

Idiomatic Meaning: Better is to bow then breake.

Egri köchettin egri derex chiqar.

A crooked twig begets a crooked tree.

Idiomatic Meaning: As the twig is bent, so is the tree inclined.

El razi xuda razi.
People's satisfaction is God's satisfaction.
Literal Meaning: It emphasises the importance of valuing and prioritising the satisfaction and well-being of others. It suggests that kindness and compassion towards people are socially desirable and aligned with spiritual or moral values.

Elchige ölüm yoq.
There is no death for a messenger.
Idiomatic Meaning: Don't shoot the messenger.

Ëlimchi arslan, bërimchi chashqan.
The taker is the lion, and the giver is the mouse. (Kashgari 1072–74)
Literal Meaning: It contrasts confident promises made when borrowing and hesitant actions when it comes time to return. It emphasises the importance of integrity, fulfilling commitments, and the consequences of failing.

Elning sözi xudaning sözi.
People's word is God's word.
Idiomatic Meaning: The voice of the people is the voice of God.

Emili yoq sopidin[2] tuxumi yoq toxu yaxshi.
An eggless chicken surpasses a powerless Sufi.
Idiomatic Meaning: Better are small fish than an empty dish.

Eqil - idrak qeyerde bolsa, ulughluq shu yerde bolidu.
Where there is wisdom, there is greatness.
Idiomatic Meaning: Where bees are, there is honey.

---

[2] a Muslim who represents the mystical dimension of Islam

Eqil tapay dëseng kitab al.
> To attain wisdom, you must invest in books.
> **Literal Meaning: It** emphasises the active pursuit of
> knowledge and the investment in educational resources to
> acquire wisdom. It underscores the importance of self-
> directed learning and recognises that wisdom is attainable
> through personal effort and engagement with educational
> materials.

Eqil tapay dëseng ögen.
> To seek wisdom, you must embrace learning.
> **Literal Meaning: It** emphasises the active pursuit of
> knowledge and the importance of continuous learning in
> the journey towards wisdom. It highlights the need for
> curiosity, open-mindedness, and a commitment to
> ongoing personal growth and development.

Eqil yashta emes bashta.
> Wisdom does not lie in age but in the mind.
> **Idiomatic Meaning:** Wisdom doesn't come with age.

Eqilge isharet nadangha juwalduruz.
> A sign is enough to the wise.
> **Literal Meaning: It** highlights wise individuals'
> perceptive nature and ability to understand and respond to
> subtle indications or cues. It underscores the importance
> of effective communication, both verbal and nonverbal,
> and the influence it can have on those who possess
> wisdom.

Eqilning közi bolmisa, köz dëgen tam tüshüki.
> Without the eye of wisdom, the eye is but a hollow in the
> wall.
> **Literal Meaning: It** implies that mere physical sight is
> meaningless without the ability to perceive and
> understand things deeply. It emphasises the importance of
> wisdom and insight in truly gaining knowledge and
> making sense of the world. Without wisdom, our

perception is shallow and lacks true understanding,
rendering it as insignificant as a hole in the wall.

Er bëshigha kün kelse, ötük bilen su këcher.
When a man needs it, he drinks water from his boots.
Idiomatic Meaning: Needs must when the devil drives.

Erdem bashi til.
In the realm of virtue, language takes the lead. (Kashgari
1072–74)
Literal Meaning: It conveys how a person speaks and
communicates, reflecting their character and moral
values. It suggests that an individual's words and language
can reveal their true nature, integrity, and virtuous
qualities. Just as a mirror reflects one's physical
appearance, a person's language reflects their inner
virtues, providing insights into their honesty, kindness,
wisdom, and other positive attributes.

Erdemsizdin qut këtidu.
A man without virtue loses the company of happiness.
(Kashgari 1072–74)
Literal Meaning: It expresses that moral goodness and
virtuous behaviour are essential for experiencing true
happiness and contentment in life. When a person lacks
integrity, honesty, kindness, and other virtuous qualities,
they become disconnected from genuine happiness and
find it difficult to sustain a fulfilling and joyful existence.
Virtue is a guiding principle, allowing individuals to
cultivate meaningful relationships, inner peace, and a
sense of purpose, ultimately leading to lasting happiness.

Ërinchekke bosughimu dawan köründer .
for the lazy, even a sill becomes a hill. (Kashgari 1072–
74)
Literal Meaning: It conveys that an idle person may
perceive even small tasks as significant obstacles due to
their lack of motivation and effort. It serves as a reminder

of the importance of diligence, action, and a proactive approach to tasks and responsibilities.

Ërinchekke bulut kölenggisi yuk bolur.

For a lazy, cloud shadows are a burden. (Kashgari 1072–74)

Literal Meaning: This proverb implies that those who are lazy or idle find even the most minor tasks or responsibilities to be burdensome and overwhelming. Like the passing shadows cast by clouds, which are temporary and fleeting, the idler sees ordinary or manageable activities as obstacles or sources of difficulty. It highlights the contrast between someone who lacks motivation or a strong work ethic and those who embrace productivity and actively engage in their pursuits. The proverb serves as a reminder of the consequences of laziness and the importance of taking initiative and responsibility to lead a fulfilling and purposeful life.

Ërinchekning etisi tügimes.

Idlers tomorrow never comes.

Literal Meaning: A lazy person often pushes things off to the next day, promising to do them later, but that day never arrives. It highlights the consequences of laziness and the tendency to delay necessary actions or tasks. It encourages individuals to overcome idleness and take immediate action to accomplish their goals and responsibilities to avoid a perpetually postponed future.

Erke ösken bala, bolidu ishqa chala.

A spoiled child is good for nothing.

Literal Meaning: This proverb conveys that a child who is excessively indulged, pampered, or given everything they desire without effort or responsibility tends to grow up lacking essential skills, resilience, and the ability to contribute meaningfully to society. Such a child becomes accustomed to having their wishes granted without understanding the value of hard work, perseverance, and personal development. As a result, they may need help to face challenges, take initiative, or achieve success independently. The proverb serves as a reminder of the importance of instilling discipline, responsibility, and a strong work ethic in children to help them become capable and productive individuals in adulthood.

Erni er qilghanmu xotun, erni yer qilghanmu xotun.
A good wife makes a good husband.
Idiomatic Meaning: Two things prolong your life: a quiet heart and a loving wife.

Erning gheyriti, taghni qum qilar.
Man's determination turns mountains into sand.
Idiomatic Meaning: Faith will move mountains.

Erning sözi bir, ëgerning köki üch.
Man's words are one, and a saddle's thread is three. (Kashgari 1072–74)
Literal Meaning: It underscores the importance of honesty, consistency, and reliability in communication. It suggests that a person's words should be firm, unwavering, and aligned with their actions. By maintaining the integrity of their speech, individuals can establish trust and credibility in their relationships and interactions with others.

Erzan göshning shorpisi tëtimas.
Cheap meat never makes good broth.
Literal Meaning: It warns against compromising on quality and value. It suggests that using low-quality or inexpensive ingredients will result in an inferior outcome, whether in cooking or other areas of life. It encourages individuals to prioritise quality and make conscious choices, leading to more fulfilling and satisfactory results.

Eski bilen gep talashqiche, It bilen söngek talashqan yaxshi.
It is better to argue with a dog for a bone than to involve

oneself with an evil man.

Literal Meaning: This proverb highlights that engaging in conflicts or disputes with malicious or wicked individuals is more detrimental than engaging in minor conflicts over material possessions. The proverb suggests that avoiding engaging with individuals with ill intentions is wiser, as they are more likely to cause harm and create unnecessary trouble. It implies that it is better to choose our battles wisely, focusing on protecting our well-being and avoiding unnecessary confrontations with those who have malicious intent. By emphasising the importance of discernment and prioritising one's peace of mind, the proverb reminds us to be cautious in choosing our conflicts and avoid unnecessary entanglements with individuals who may bring negativity into our lives.

Eski chapanning ichide er bar.

Beneath a tattered coat resides a gentleman.

Literal Meaning: It conveys that one's true character and nobility are not defined by material possessions or social status. It emphasises valuing individuals based on their inner qualities, virtues, and actions rather than their external appearances. It encourages empathy, open-mindedness, and a deeper understanding of others, reminding us that true greatness and worthiness can be found in unexpected places.

Et tirnaqtin ayrilmas.

The flesh cannot be separated from the nails. (Kashgari 1072–74)

Literal Meaning: It can be applied to various contexts. For example, it can be used to describe the close bond between family members, where the ties are so strong that they cannot be easily severed. It can also express the interconnectedness of different aspects of a complex system, where altering one component can have ripple effects on the entire system. It highlights that some things are inherently connected and cannot be easily separated, underscoring the importance of recognising and understanding the interdependencies and interconnectedness in various aspects of life.

Etiki quyruqtin bügünki öpke yaxshi.
Today's sheep lungs are better than tomorrow's sheep tail.
Idiomatic Meaning: Better an egg today than a hen tomorrow; a bird in the hand is worth two in the bush; fifty percent of something is better than one hundred percent of nothing.

Exlaq adem zinniti.
Virtue is the beautiful adornment of a person.
Literal Meaning: This proverb suggests true beauty lies in possessing virtuous qualities rather than superficial or materialistic attributes. It promotes the notion that individuals should prioritise developing their inner virtues and ethical behaviour, as these qualities contribute to their overall appeal and make them genuinely admirable. It highlights the significance of character and integrity in defining a person's true beauty, which transcends physical appearances alone.

Exmeq chong-kichiki yoq.
A fool comes in all sizes.
Literal Meaning: The proverb implies that foolishness or lack of wisdom is not limited to physical appearance, age, or stature. It suggests that individuals can exhibit foolish behaviour regardless of their outward characteristics or social status. It serves as a reminder that foolishness is not exclusive to a specific group of people. It suggests that one should not make assumptions about a person's intelligence or character solely based on external appearances. It encourages individuals to look beyond superficial factors and evaluate others based on their actions, decisions, and behaviours rather than physical attributes.

Exmeq elchi ikki terepni buzar.
A foolish apostle will destroy both sides.
Literal Meaning: It emphasises the importance of having wise and knowledgeable individuals in positions of leadership or influence. It suggests that decisions made by someone lacking wisdom can lead to harm, conflict, or negative consequences for all parties involved. It serves as a reminder to consider the qualifications, wisdom, and character of individuals who hold positions of influence, as their actions and choices can have far-reaching impacts. It highlights the significance of wisdom, discernment, and thoughtful decision-making, cautioning against the negative effects that can arise when a foolish or unwise person assumes a position of influence.

Exmeqning chong - kichiki bolmas.
Fools are not defined by their age.
Idiomatic Meaning: A fool at forty is a fool indeed.

Exmeqning qoli uzun, eqli qisqa.
Fool's hands are long, but his mind is short.
Idiomatic Meaning: A fool and his money are soon parted.

Gepdan bolghuche ishchan bol.
Work hard instead of being talkative.
Literal Meaning: It emphasises the value of action and productivity over mere talk or empty words. It suggests that it is more important to focus on putting in effort and achieving tangible results through hard work rather than simply making loud declarations or boasting about one's abilities. By prioritising action and productivity, individuals can demonstrate their capabilities and achieve success through their accomplishments rather than relying solely on words or empty promises. Ultimately, this mindset encourages individuals to let their actions speak for themselves and to channel their energy into

meaningful work rather than engaging in excessive talk or empty rhetoric.

Ghalcha at minse chiqmighan döngi qalmas, dëdek munchaq assa kirmigen öyi qalmas.
Give a sycophant wings, and they will soar beyond their realm; adorn a servant with jewels, and they will explore every corner of their realm.
Idiomatic Meaning: Set a beggar on horseback, and he'll ride to the devil; Put a beggar on horseback and he'll ride it to death.

Ghaz topi bashlamchisiz bolmas.
Gaggle cannot be leaderless. (Kashgari 1072–74)
Literal Meaning: It serves as a reminder of the importance of leadership in any collective endeavour. It implies that the group's progress, unity, and effectiveness may be compromised without a leader or someone to take on that role. It emphasises the significance of leadership in maintaining order, direction, and cohesiveness within a group. It suggests that effective leadership is essential for the success and productivity of any collective effort.

Ghem ömürni yeydu.
Grief consumes life.
Idiomatic Meaning: Fretting cares make grey hairs.

Güldüri bar, yamghuri yoq.
There is thunder but no rain.
Idiomatic Meaning: big thunder, little rain.

Haya bilen exlaq, acha bilen singil.
Modesty and morality are sisters.
Literal Meaning: The proverb "modesty and morality are brother and sister" highlights the strong connection and interdependence between the virtues of modesty and morality. Modesty refers to being humble, unassuming, and free from excessive pride or arrogance. It involves having a moderate and reserved demeanour, particularly

regarding one's achievements, appearance, or behaviour. Conversely, morality refers to adherence to ethical principles, standards, or codes of conduct. It encompasses distinguishing between right and wrong and making decisions based on principles of fairness, justice, and integrity. By describing modesty and morality as "brother and sister," the proverb suggests that these virtues are closely related and go hand in hand. They are seen as complementary qualities that reinforce and support each other. Modesty helps to keep one grounded and humble, preventing moral lapses due to arrogance or self-centeredness. At the same time, morality guides and directs modesty by providing a moral compass and ensuring that one's actions align with ethical principles. In principle, this proverb emphasises the importance of both modesty and morality in leading a virtuous and upright life, highlighting their intertwined nature and their positive influence on one another.

Haya ketse bala këlur.

When modesty departs, misfortune draws near.
Literal Meaning: It underscores the belief that immodest behaviours or the absence of modesty can invite negative consequences or unfortunate events. It encourages individuals to cultivate and uphold modesty as a virtue to foster harmonious relationships and avoid unnecessary misfortunes in life.

Hayat cheklik, bilim cheksiz.

Life has its limits, while knowledge knows no bounds.
Idiomatic Meaning: Art is long and life is short.

Hayat qisqa.

Life is short.
Idiomatic Meaning: Life is too short.

Hayatliq - herikette.

Life finds its essence in action.

Literal Meaning: It reminds us that active participation and initiative are fundamental to living a purposeful and enriching life. It encourages individuals to embrace opportunities, overcome challenges, and actively shape their destinies rather than simply being passive observers or bystanders in life's journey.

Hemme ish yoli bilen, kona tammu uli bilen.
There is measure in all things; the old wall is its base.
Idiomatic Meaning: there is measure in all things.

Her gülning özige chüshlüq puriqi bar,.
Each flower has its smell.
Idiomatic Meaning: Aach to his own taste.

Her kim qilsa, özige qilar.
What you do to others returns to yourself.
Idiomatic Meaning: As you sow, so shall you reap; every herring must hang by its own gill.

Her kimning qedri öz qolida.
Everyone's destiny is in their own hands.
Idiomatic Meaning: Every man is the architect of his own fortune.

Her kimning qimmiti bar.
Everyone has value.
Idiomatic Meaning: Every man has his price.

Her kimning söygini özige chirayliq.
Everyone's lover is beautiful.
Idiomatic Meaning: Every man to his taste.

Heriket qilsang beriket taparsen, ixlas qilsang meripet taparsen,.
Actions open the door to flourishing; sincerity lights the path to enlightenment.
Idiomatic Meaning: Seek and you shall find.

Herkim öz ölüki üchün yighlar.
Every heart knows its sorrow.
Literal Meaning: It reflects the profound and personal nature of contemplating one's mortality and acknowledges the natural tendency to prioritise our own lives. It serves as a reminder to value and cherish our existence while also recognising the universal experience of mortality that we all share.

Herqanche exmeq bolsimu, hemrah yaxshi, herqanche egri bolsimu, yol yaxshi.
No matter how foolish, a companion is good; no matter how crooked, the road is good. (Kashgari 1072–74)
Literal Meaning: It highlights the significance of companionship and the ability to find goodness and positivity in people and situations, regardless of their perceived shortcomings or imperfections. It reminds us that the presence of others and the journey hold inherent value, regardless of any perceived flaws or challenges.
Opposite in English: Better to be alone than in bad company.

Heselning herisi bar, gülning tikini.
A bee has a sting; a flower has a thorn.
Idiomatic Meaning: No rose without a thorn; every rose has its thorn.

Hile bilen arslan tutular, küch bilen qaranchuqmu tutulmas.
Craftiness may snare a lion, yet force cannot conquer a scarecrow. (Kashgari 1072–74)
Literal Meaning: It highlights the importance of using the appropriate approach or strategy when dealing with different circumstances or individuals. It acknowledges that not all challenges or adversaries can be tackled similarly. Sometimes, a clever and strategic approach is required to overcome a formidable opponent, whereas a less significant or threatening entity may be handled

straightforwardly. The proverb emphasises the significance of adaptability and intelligence in dealing with various situations. It suggests that understanding the nature of the challenge or adversary and employing the right strategy is crucial for achieving success.

Hinggaymisa dinggaymaydu.
If one doesn't smile, they won't be approached.
Idiomatic Meaning: There is always one who kisses, and one who turns the cheek.

Horunning etisi tola.
A lazy man always has plenty of tomorrows.
Literal Meaning: This proverb serves as a cautionary reminder about the consequences of laziness and procrastination. It encourages individuals to be proactive, diligent, and responsible in tackling their obligations rather than continually pushing them off indefinitely. It highlights the importance of acting in the present moment and avoiding the trap of constantly relying on "tomorrow" as an excuse for inaction.

Ikki at tëpisher, arida qalghan ëshek öler.
While the two horses fight, the donkey suffers.
Literal Meaning: It implies the senselessness or futility of inevitable conflicts, as it portrays the harm inflicted on an innocent party. It encourages individuals to consider the wider impact of their actions and disputes and to strive for peaceful resolutions that minimise damage to others. The proverb underscores the importance of considering the broader consequences and being mindful of the potential harm that can arise during conflicts, emphasising the value of empathy, peaceful resolutions, and minimising collateral damage.

Ikki bughra ekisher, arida köküyün yanjilar.
While two male camels fight, the gadfly dies. (Kashgari

1072–74)
*see **Ikki at tëpisher, arida qalghan ëshek öler***.

Ikki qagha poq talashsa, owchigha payda.
When the crows fight, the hunter will delight.
Idiomatic Meaning: While two dogs are fighting for a bone, a third runs away with it.

Ikki qoshqar soqushsa itqa ozuq chiqar.
While two rams fight, the dog runs away with the bone.
Idiomatic Meaning: While two dogs are fighting for a bone, a third runs away with it.

Ikki qoshqarning bëshi bir qazanda pishmas.
The heads of two sheep cannot fit within a single pot. (Kashgari 1072–74)
Literal Meaning: The proverb can also be applied to situations where trying to satisfy multiple conflicting interests or expectations may lead to frustration, disappointment, or failure. It encourages individuals to prioritise and make realistic and compatible choices rather than trying to achieve conflicting objectives simultaneously. It serves as a reminder to consider the inherent limitations and contradictions in certain situations and to make practical choices based on that awareness. It emphasises the need for realistic expectations and the understanding that some goals or desires may be incompatible or mutually exclusive.

Ikki tawuzni bir qoltuqqa qisqili bolmas, ikki këmige teng dessigili bolmas.
An armpit cannot hold two watermelons, and a foot cannot stand on two boats simultaneously.
Idiomatic Meaning: If you run after two hares, you will catch neither.

Im bilse, er[3] *ölmes* .

 If the private knows the password, he shall not perish.
(Kashgari 1072–74)
Literal Meaning: It highlights the importance of
knowledge and awareness as a means of self-preservation
and protection. It encourages individuals to seek
information, learn, and stay informed to navigate life's
challenges more effectively and minimise potential risks
or negative consequences.

Iparliq xaltidin ipar ketse, hidi qalar.
If the musk is removed from the bag, its fragrance
permeates the air. (Kashgari 1072–74)
Literal Meaning: It reminds us that the consequences or
effects of something or someone can persist long after
their physical presence is gone. It underscores the idea
that certain influences or qualities can leave a lasting
mark on people or situations, even if the source is no
longer present.

Ish ömlükte, küch birlikte.
Work thrives in unity; power flourishes in togetherness.
Idiomatic Meaning: Union is strength.

Ish peytide, sodiger paydida.
Work is better on its time; the trader is at a profit.
(Kashgari 1072–74)
Literal Meaning: The proverb underscores that work or
effort invested at the right time is more likely to yield
fruitful results. It implies that aligning one's actions with
favourable conditions or circumstances can contribute to
overall success and productivity. It encourages individuals
to recognise the significance of timing in their work and
endeavours. It advises them to consider the optimal time

---

[3] a private soldier is the lowest ranked soldier.

for action and planning, as doing so can lead to favourable
outcomes and increase the chances of success.

Ishligen chishleydu, ishlimigen chishlimeydu.
The worked bite, the unworked fades.
Idiomatic Meaning: If you won't work you shan't eat.

Ishtini pütün xalighan yërige olturar.
If the pants are fine, you can sit anywhere with ease.
(Kashgari 1072–74)
Literal Meaning: The proverb encourages individuals to
prioritise preparedness, self-improvement, and being well-
equipped in different aspects of life. It suggests that by
investing time and effort into personal development and
acquiring the necessary skills or knowledge, individuals
can enhance their ability to handle diverse circumstances
and make the most of them. It promotes being prepared,
adaptable, and ready to face different situations. It
highlights the value of having the necessary resources or
skills to navigate life's challenges and opportunities
comfortably.

Isliq öyüm, issiq öyüm.
My smoky house, my warm house.
Idiomatic Meaning: Home is home, as the devil said
when he found himself in the court of session.

Israpchiliq - xarabliq.
Waste breeds devastation.
Literal Meaning: It reminds us to be conscientious,
resourceful, and prudent in our actions and decisions. It
encourages individuals to value and appreciate what they
have, use resources efficiently, and avoid wasteful
practices that can have detrimental effects. Individuals
can contribute to a more sustainable and prosperous future
by embracing a conservation mindset and responsible
behaviour.

It - itliqini qilmisa köngli tinmas.
Dog's habits are set in stone.
Idiomatic Meaning: The dog returns to its vomit.

It chishlimes, at tepmes dëme.
Never assume a dog will not bite or a horse will not kick.
(Kashgari 1072–74)
Literal Meaning: The proverb encourages individuals to approach situations with a healthy level of scepticism and to avoid making hasty judgments or underestimating potential risks. It reminds us that even seemingly harmless entities or individuals can display unexpected or unfavourable behaviour under certain circumstances. It cautions against complacency, encourages vigilance, and promotes a realistic and discerning mindset when assessing the behaviour and intentions of both animals and people.

It hürer, karwan yürer.
Dog barks, and the caravan goes on.
Idiomatic Meaning: dogs bark, but the caravan goes on.

Itning aghzidin söngek ashmas, gheywetxorning aghzidin gep (ashmas)
Both a dog and a gossip cling tightly to their bones.
Idiomatic Meaning: A dog that will fetch a bone will carry a bone.

Itqa nan berse qolini chishleptu.
He gave the dog bread, and it bit his hand.
Idiomatic Meaning: Take an old, dirty, hungry, mangy, sick and wet dog and feed him and wash him and nurse him back to health, and he will never turn on you and bite you. This is how man and dog differ.

Ittin qorqqan abdal bolmaptu.
He who is afraid of dogs cannot be a beggar.
Idiomatic Meaning: If you can't take the heat, get out of the kitchen.

Ittipaqliq küch.
>Unity is strength.
>**Idiomatic Meaning:** Unity is strength.

Jan ësen bolsa, tangqalarliq ishlarni köp körer.
>If you are alive, you will witness many wonders.
>(Kashgari 1072–74)
>**Literal Meaning:** The proverb reminds us that life is full
>of surprises and that staying engaged and receptive to the
>world around us makes us more likely to encounter
>strange and remarkable phenomena that enrich our
>experiences and broaden our perspectives.

Jandin kechmigiche janan'gha yetkili bolmas.
>Without sacrifice, beauty remains elusive.
>**Idiomatic Meaning:** faint heart ne'er won fair lady.

Jan'gha jan, qan'gha qan.
>Soul for soul, blood for blood.
>**Idiomatic Meaning:** an eye for an eye and a tooth for a
>tooth.

Japa tartmay halawet yoq, inaq ötmey sa'adet (yoq)
>There is no happiness without hardship and no pleasure
>without harmony.
>**Idiomatic Meaning:** no pain, no gain; nothing ventured,
>nothing gain.

Jigdidin badam chiqmas, bilimlik kishidin nadan (chiqmas)
>Oleaster cannot be almond; wise cannot be irrational.
>**Idiomatic Meaning:** You can't make a silk purse out of a
>sow's ear.

Jimghurning hüniri ichide.
>The craft of silent man is hidden within.
>**Idiomatic Meaning:** A clever hawk hides its claws; a still
>tongue makes a wise head.

Kemter bolsang ösersen, meghrurlansang chökersen.
If you are humble, you will rise; if you are proud, you will sink.
Idiomatic Meaning: Pride comes before a fall.

Këngeshlik ish buzulmas.
Counselled work will not go wrong. (Kashgari 1072–74)
Literal Meaning: When you seek and follow sound advice or guidance while working on something, the chances of making mistakes or facing significant issues are significantly reduced. This proverb highlights the importance of consulting knowledgeable or experienced individuals to achieve successful outcomes.

Këngeshlik ish üzlishar, këngeshsiz ish buzular.
Work with counsel finds resolution; work without it faces a struggle. (Kashgari 1072–74)
Idiomatic Meaning: Trouble shared is trouble halved.

Këpil bolghuche, ot tut.
Better to catch fire than be a guarantor. (Kashgari 1072–74)
Literal Meaning: It encourages individuals to prioritise their well-being and avoid putting themselves at risk by taking on excessive obligations for others. It serves as a reminder to consider the potential consequences before agreeing to be a guarantor and to be cautious when assuming financial or legal responsibilities for someone else.

Këreklik tashning ëghiri yoq.
A helpful stone never feels heavy.
Idiomatic Meaning: Keep a thing seven years and you'll always find a use for it.

Këselge qarap dora, kanggha qarap mora.
Match the remedy to the ailment and the chimney to the stove.

Idiomatic Meaning: Circumstances alter cases; cut your coat according to your cloth.

Këselni yoshursang, ölümi ashkare.
Conceal the ailment, and the truth of mortality shall be unveiled.
Idiomatic Meaning: Love and a cough cannot be hid.

Këselning anisi zukam.
The mother of the disease is influenza.
Literal Meaning: By referring to influenza as the "mother of disease," the statement underscores its capacity to initiate or contribute to the occurrence of other diseases. It underscores the contrasting nature of influenza as a disease-causing agent.

Kichik balini ishqa buyrusang, arqisidin özüng bar.
When you assign a task to a child, you must follow up.
Idiomatic Meaning: Never send a boy to do a man's job.

Kichikide qattiq tirishsa, chong bolghanda söyüner.
Sow diligence in youth to reap happiness in adulthood. (Kashgari 1072–74)
Literal Meaning: By investing time and effort in personal development during youth, individuals may be more likely to achieve their goals, fulfil their potential, and lead a satisfying life as they grow older. It can lay the groundwork for future success, whether in education, career, relationships, or personal well-being. While hard work is important, finding a balance and caring for one's well-being is essential. Pursuing passions, maintaining healthy relationships, and prioritising self-care alongside hard work is crucial to ensure overall happiness and fulfilment in life.

Kim tütün qopursa, özi islinur.
He who raises the smoke shall bear the burn (Kashgari 1072–74)
Literal Meaning: The proverb serves as a cautionary

reminder that dishonesty, manipulation, and deceit rarely lead to positive outcomes in the long run. It encourages individuals to embrace honesty, integrity, and transparency in their dealings with others. By doing so, they can foster trust, build stronger relationships, and avoid the negative consequences associated with deceptive behaviour. The proverb highlights that actions have consequences and that engaging in dishonest or manipulative behaviour can ultimately lead to one's downfall or harm.

Kimning gëpini qilsa shu keptu.
Talk about the man, and he is bound to appear.
Idiomatic Meaning: Talk of the devil, and he is bound to appear; talk of the devil and he's sure to appear.

Kimning yënida qashtëshi bolsa, uninggha chaqmaq tegmeydu.
Those adorned with jade need not fear the lightning's blade. (Kashgari 1072–74)
Literal Meaning: This proverb implies that possessing a protective charm or being in a favourable position can shield a person from harm or misfortune. In this case, having jade symbolises good fortune or protection, suggesting that one who possesses jade will be safe from lightning strikes. It highlights having something valuable or advantageous to safeguard against potential dangers.

Kishi menggü yashimas, görge kirse arqigha yanmas.
A man cannot live forever; once in the grave, he never returns. (Kashgari 1072–74)
Literal Meaning: It reminds us of the finite nature of human life and encourages individuals to live purposefully and fully in the time they have. It highlights the importance of cherishing and making the most of our mortal existence.

Kishi sözliship, haywan hidliship.
People are known through words, while animals recognise
through scent. (Kashgari 1072–74)
Literal Meaning: This proverb highlights the different
methods of communication and recognition between
humans and animals. Humans rely on verbal
communication to get to know one another, share
information, and build connections. On the other hand,
animals often rely on their keen sense of smell to identify
and familiarise themselves with other members of their
species. It underscores the distinct ways different beings
establish familiarity and understanding within their
respective realms of existence.

Kishining eyibini kolighuche, özüngning burnini kola.
Better to pick your nose than to pick fault in others.
Literal Meaning: This proverb suggests that it is more
acceptable or preferable to focus on addressing one's
flaws or shortcomings rather than constantly criticising or
finding fault in others. It implies that self-reflection and
self-improvement should take precedence over being
overly critical or judgmental towards others. It
emphasises the importance of personal accountability and
growth rather than engaging in negative or unproductive
behaviour such as excessive fault-finding.

Kiyim ademning zinniti, iger atning (zinniti)
Clothes embellish a man, while a saddle adorns a horse.
Idiomatic Meaning: clothes maketh the man.

Kökke tükürse yüzige chüsher.
He who spits at the sky shall find it falling upon his face.
(Kashgari 1072–74)
Literal Meaning: This proverb conveys that any negative
or harmful action one directs outwardly will eventually
have consequences that come back to affect them
personally. It serves as a metaphorical warning against
engaging in disrespectful, offensive, or spiteful actions

towards others. The imagery of spitting at the sky illustrates the futility of such actions, as they are bound to rebound and cause harm to oneself. It encourages individuals to consider their behaviour's repercussions and treat others with respect and kindness.

Köp izdenseng eqil taparsen.
Study cultivates wisdom within the mind.
Literal Meaning: This proverb emphasises the transformative power of education and learning. It suggests that one can develop wisdom and intellectual maturity through diligent study and acquiring knowledge. It highlights the importance of continuous learning and intellectual growth in shaping a person's understanding and decision-making abilities. The proverb encourages individuals to prioritise education and the pursuit of knowledge to develop wisdom and broaden their perspectives.

Köp söyünüp ketse, qattiq öküner.
Excessive excitement paves the way to regret. (Kashgari 1072–74)
Literal Meaning: This proverb cautions against allowing oneself to become overly excited or carried away. It suggests that when one indulges in excessive enthusiasm or fervour without proper consideration, it often leads to subsequent regret or disappointment. It emphasises the importance of maintaining a balanced and measured approach, avoiding extreme emotions or impulsive actions that may later result in negative consequences. The proverb serves as a reminder to exercise moderation and prudence in dealing with situations to minimise the chances of regretting one's actions or decisions.

Köp uxlisang ach qalisen.
Too much sleep leads to hunger.
Literal Meaning: This proverb implies that if a person spends excessive amounts of time sleeping instead of

engaging in productive activities, they may need more
means to obtain food, which can ultimately lead to
hunger. It highlights the importance of maintaining a
balanced sleep and work.

Köpning eqli köp.
> Amidst many, wisdom thrives.
> **Idiomatic Meaning:** Many hands make light work; so
> many heads, so many wits; two heads are better than one.

Köpning küchi köp.
> Strength lies in numbers.
> **Idiomatic Meaning:** Many hands make light work; when
> spider webs unite, they can tie up a lion.

Köpning küchi tagh kötirer.
> Where many unite, mountains can be moved.
> **Idiomatic Meaning:** many hands make light work.

Köpning küchige, taghmu teng këlelmes.
> Even a mountain bows to the might of many.
> **Idiomatic Meaning:** when spider webs unite, they can tie
> up a lion.

Körün'gen tagh yiraq emes.
> The mountain in sight is not far.
> **Literal Meaning:** By emphasising the visibility of the
> mountain, the proverb encourages individuals to have a
> clear vision, set specific goals, and pursue them with
> determination. It suggests that when you can see what you
> want to achieve, it becomes more tangible, and you are
> more likely to take the necessary steps to reach it.

Köterse geden'ge miniptu.
> Having been raised with respect, he mounted on the back
> of the one who nurtured him.
> **Idiomatic Meaning:** Familiarity breeds contempt.

Köz körmise, köngül söymeydu.
If the eye does not see, the heart does not love.
Idiomatic Meaning: what the eye doesn't see, the heart doesn't grieve over.

Közdin yiraq, köngüldin yiraq.
Out of sight, out of mind. (Kashgari 1072–74)
Idiomatic Meaning: Out of sight, out of mind.

Közge ilmighan chomaq qangsharni yarar.
A neglected stick may break the head.
Literal Meaning: This proverb emphasises the potential harm that can arise from neglecting or underestimating seemingly insignificant or overlooked things. It suggests that even a seemingly unimportant object, like a stick, can cause significant damage or harm if not given proper attention or consideration. It serves as a reminder not to disregard or underestimate any potential source of danger or harm, as even small or overlooked things can have unexpected consequences. The proverb highlights the importance of attentiveness and taking precautions to prevent avoidable accidents or mishaps.

Közi körmigen qarighu emes, xet tonumighan qarighu.
It is not the blind who lack sight but the blind who lack knowledge of letters.
Idiomatic Meaning: there's none so blind as those who will not see.

Kül püwligüche, chogh püwligen tüzük.
It's better to blow fire than to blow ashes. (Kashgari 1072–74)
Literal Meaning: This proverb implies that it is more productive and beneficial to focus on generating new ideas, energy, or enthusiasm rather than dwelling on past accomplishments or dwelling in stagnation. Blowing fire symbolises creating something new, vibrant, and impactful, while blowing ashes represents focusing on

things that have already lost their vitality or significance.
The proverb encourages individuals to prioritise
innovation, growth, and forward momentum rather than
getting stuck in complacency or dwelling on past
achievements that may no longer hold value. It highlights
the importance of staying active, passionate, and
continuously seeking new opportunities for progress and
success.

Künde yëriq yoq, begde yëniwëlish yoq.
There is no crack in the sun nor break in the gentlemen's
promise. (Kashgari 1072–74)
Literal Meaning: This proverb conveys the idea of
unwavering integrity and reliability. It suggests that just
as the sun remains whole and unbroken, a true gentleman
or honourable person keeps their promises and
commitments without fail. It emphasises the steadfastness
and trustworthiness of someone who upholds their word
and maintains their integrity. The proverb serves as a
reminder of the importance of honouring commitments
and acting with integrity, highlighting the value of trust
and dependability in personal and professional
relationships.

Küzning qandaq këlishi yazdin melum bolidu.
Autumn reveals itself through the traces of summer.
(Kashgari 1072–74)
Literal Meaning: Metaphorically, the proverb can be
applied to various aspects of life. It implies that one can
gain insights into what may happen by paying attention to
the signs, patterns, or indicators in a particular situation or
context. It encourages observation, attentiveness, and
recognising the early signs of impending change or
developments. The proverb reminds us to be mindful of
the clues and signals around us, as they can provide
valuable information about what lies ahead. We can make
more informed decisions and preparations for the future
by paying attention to the present.

Mal igisini dorimisa haram.
It is haram[4] if it does not resemble its master.
Idiomatic Meaning: like father, like son; like mother, like daughter.

Mal türi bilen, adem xili bilen.
Goods flock together by their kind, people by their kind.
Idiomatic Meaning: birds of a feather flock together.

Maxtap qoysa malxiyigha chiqiriptu.
When praised, his ego overflows like a running river.
Idiomatic Meaning: The higher the monkey climbs, the more he shows his tail.

Meghrurlansang chökersen.
Where pride abounds, the fall awaits.
Idiomatic Meaning: Pride comes before the fall.

Mëhman kelse qut këler.
When the guest arrives, joy walks through the door (Kashgari 1072–74)
Literal Meaning: This proverb conveys the idea that the arrival of a guest brings happiness and delight. It suggests that the presence of a visitor or guest adds a special spark and enhances the overall atmosphere or mood. The proverb emphasises the importance of hospitality, welcoming others into our lives, and creating an inviting environment. It reflects the notion that the company of others can bring joy and a sense of fulfilment. The proverb serves as a reminder to appreciate and cherish our connections and interactions with guests or visitors, as they can enrich our lives and bring happiness to both parties involved.

Mëhnetning tëgi rahet.
The foundation of labour is comfort.

---

[4] Anything that is forbidden or prohibited by Islamic law.

Idiomatic Meaning: Crosses are ladders that lead to heaven.

Men qilarmen ottuz, xudayim qilar toqquz.
I do thirty; God does nine.
Idiomatic Meaning: every man for himself, and God for us all.

Mergen atqan oqdin biliner.
A sniper is known for his shot.
Idiomatic Meaning: A carpenter is known by his chips.

Mergen oqyasi bilen emes, mergenliki bilen dangliq.
An archer's renown rests on their aim, not their bow.
Literal Meaning: While having quality tools and resources can certainly contribute to one's abilities, the proverb reminds us that the individual's mastery and accomplishment ultimately matter most. It encourages us to focus on honing our skills, improving our performance, and delivering excellent results rather than relying solely on external factors. The proverb can be applied to various aspects of life, emphasising the value of personal capabilities, expertise, and achievements over superficial attributes or external appearances. It serves as a reminder to recognise and appreciate individuals' true essence and capabilities rather than being overly influenced by external factors or material possessions.

Mertem mertem üch mertem.
Try three times; the third attempt brings luck.
Idiomatic Meaning: third time lucky.

Mëwilik derex ëgilip turidu, kishiler anga tërek qoyidu.
Mëwisiz derex ghadiyip turidu, kishiler uni putap turidu.
Fruitful trees bow, gaining support; fruitless trees stand tall, facing the axe.
Idiomatic Meaning: The nail that sticks up will be hammered down.

Mëwisiz derexni qaqma, gumanliq yerde yatma.
Do not shake fruitless trees nor rest in dubious spaces.
Literal Meaning: The proverb promotes the importance of making wise decisions, selecting fruitful opportunities, and aligning oneself with trustworthy and worthwhile endeavours. It encourages individuals to prioritise productivity, integrity, and certainty in their pursuits and avoid investing in or being associated with things or situations that lack value or carry unnecessary risks. By following this advice, one can focus on meaningful and fruitful endeavours, cultivate positive relationships, and safeguard themselves against unnecessary risks or disappointments. It serves as a reminder to be cautious, discerning, and purposeful in one's choices and actions.

Ming anglighandin bir körgen ela.
Seeing once is superior to hearing a thousand times.
Idiomatic Meaning: Seeing is believing.

Molla köp bolsa qoy haram bolar.
Too many mullahs spoil the meat.
Idiomatic Meaning: Too many cooks spoil the broth.

Mollamning oghli urushqaq.
The clergymen's son is belligerent.
Idiomatic Meaning: Clergymen's sons always turn out badly; the apple doesn't fall far from the tree.

Mollining dëginini qil, qilghinini qilma.
Follow the clergymen's words, not his actions.
Idiomatic Meaning: Do as i say, not as i do.

Momay usul bilmes, yërim tar der.
When grandma can't dance, she blames the dance floor. (Kashgari 1072–74)
Idiomatic Meaning: a bad workman blames his tools,.

Muhebbetke meslihetchining këriki yoq.
True love requires no counsellor.
Idiomatic Meaning: Love will find a way.

Muhebbetning desmayisi muhebbet.
The investment of love is passion.
Idiomatic Meaning: love begets love.

Müshük balisi miyanglap tughular.
From the moment of birth, kittens arrive with purrs.
(Kashgari 1072–74)
Idiomatic Meaning: the apple never falls far from the tree.

Müshük qozuqtiki chawa yaghqa tëgelmey, kishining mëli manga yarashmas der.
Unable to taste the meat, the cat declares no interest in others' fare. (Kashgari 1072–74)
Literal Meaning: It conveys the idea of sour grapes or a rationalisation for unattainable desires. It suggests that when faced with something they cannot have, individuals may downplay its value or express disinterest to cope with the unfulfilled desire. The proverb serves as a reminder that humans sometimes tend to devalue what is unattainable or out of reach to ease their longing or disappointment.t conveys the idea that some individuals may reject or devalue something simply because they cannot obtain it, even if they initially desired it.

Müshükning bir puli yoq göshke amraq.
Though penniless, the cat's heart still longs for meat.
Idiomatic Meaning: All cats love fish but hate to get their paws wet.

Muzdin su tamar.
Ice drips water. (Kashgari 1072–74)
Literal Meaning: A metaphorical statement about the influence and traits passed down from parents to their children. It suggests that children often inherit specific

characteristics or behaviours from their parents, just as water drips from melting ice. This proverb emphasises that children tend to resemble their parents in various ways.

Nabab yerge tügmen qursa, kütmigende yar këter.
A mill built on unfavourable ground is destined to drown in flood. **(Kashgari 1072–74)**
Literal Meaning: The proverb is a metaphor for the importance of careful consideration and assessment before embarking on any endeavour. It emphasises the need to choose the right environment, resources, and conditions to ensure the stability and sustainability of a project or goal. Building on a solid foundation, literally and metaphorically, is essential for long-term success and resilience. In a broader context, the proverb advises against rushing into ventures without proper evaluation or overlooking critical factors that could significantly impact the outcome. It encourages foresight, prudent decision-making, and the recognition of potential risks or weaknesses to avoid future setbacks or failures.

Nadan dosttin zërek düshmen yaxshi.
It is better to have a wise enemy than an unwise friend.
Idiomatic Meaning: better the devil you know (than the devil you don't)

Nadan tülke tumshuqidin ilinar.
A foolish fox meets its end, caught by its beak.
Idiomatic Meaning: Fools rush in where angels fear to tread.

Naxshining anisi muqam[5].
The mother of songs is muqam.

---

[5] 'Muqam' refers to a traditional musical system or style. Central Asian music is a complex form of classical music found among The Uyghur people and in Uzbekistan and Tajikistan, characterised by interconnected pieces with unique melodies and rhythms. In Islamic and Arabic contexts,

Literal Meaning: Maqam is a complex system of musical modes and structures found in the traditional music of Central Asia, particularly associated with the Uyghur people. Maqam is characterised by its intricate melodies, rhythmic patterns, and improvisational elements. By referring to maqam as the "mother of song," the statement acknowledges the rich musical heritage and the influence of this traditional form in shaping the development of songs within its cultural context. It suggests that maqam serves as a primary source or inspiration for the creation of various songs, highlighting its significance and impact on the region's musical traditions.

Nëme dëseng shuni anglaysen.
Watch your words, as they may echo back to you.
Literal Meaning: This proverb reminds us to exercise caution and thoughtfulness in our speech. It highlights the importance of considering the potential effects of our words on others and ourselves. Like an echo repeating what is spoken, our words can reverberate and influence our relationships, reputations, and overall well-being. By emphasizing the idea that our words can return to us, the proverb encourages us to choose our words wisely, speak with kindness and respect, and be aware of the power and impact of our language.

'maqam' (also spelt 'maqam') denotes melodic modes used in traditional Arabic music, each with specific rules for melody and mood. 'Uyghur Muqam' is a traditional musical form unique to the Uyghur people, primarily found in the Uyghur region. This rich musical tradition, with its elaborate compositions that include vocal and instrumental pieces, plays a central role in Uyghur cultural and social life. It uniquely reflects historical narratives and contemporary experiences, making it a vital aspect of Uyghur cultural heritage. Uyghur Muqam is characterised by its intricate melodies, rhythms, and modes, often performed with traditional instruments such as the dutar, rawap, and various types of percussion. The performances are usually elaborate, involving both solo and ensemble renditions, and they are considered a vital aspect of Uyghur cultural heritage.

Nëme tërisang shuni alisan.
The seeds you sow determine the fruits you reap.
Idiomatic Meaning: garbage in, garbage out; as you sow, so you reap; as you bake, so shall you brew; as you brew, so shall you bake; he who plants thorns should not expect to gather roses.

Nepsi yaman yette nezirdin quruq qaptu.
Greedy man lost the bite in the charity food.
Idiomatic Meaning: A bleating sheep loses a bite.

Nerse yoqatqan kishi, anisining qoyninimu axturidu.
People will search even within their mother's embrace when something is lost. (Kashgari 1072–74)
Literal Meaning: The proverb underscores emotional attachment and the extent to which one may go to find what one has lost. It reflects that people may turn to their closest and most familiar sources of comfort and support in moments of loss or adversity, seeking solace and potential solutions. Overall, the proverb portrays the deep longing and relentless search of an individual unwilling to accept a loss without exploring all possible avenues, even those that may seem improbable.

Nësidin neq yaxshi.
Cash is better than credit.
Idiomatic Meaning: A live dog is better than a dead lion.

Nesihet achchiq, mëwisi tatliq.
The counsel may be bitter, but its fruit bears sweetness.
Idiomatic Meaning: Bitter pills may have blessed effects.

Nikah - ghayib.
Marriage is luck.
Idiomatic Meaning: Marriage is a lottery.

Öchkidimu saqal bar.
The goat has a beard, too.
Idiomatic Meaning: A beard is not a sign of wisdom.

Ögen'gen xuy ölgiche.
The ingrained habit endures until death.
Idiomatic Meaning: Old habits die hard.

Oghlaq yiliksiz, bala bilimsiz bolmas.
Just as a lamb needs bone marrow, a child requires knowledge to thrive. (Kashgari 1072–74)
Literal Meaning: By highlighting the connection between bone marrow and knowledge, the proverb serves as a reminder of the indispensability of education and the value of intellectual enrichment for children. It encourages parents, educators, and society to prioritise and facilitate opportunities for children to acquire knowledge, learn new skills, and foster a lifelong love for learning. The proverb emphasises the fundamental role of knowledge in a child's growth. It underscores the importance of providing children with educational opportunities and nurturing their thirst for knowledge to enable their development and well-being.

Oghri gumanxor.
Thieves are doubters.
Idiomatic Meaning: Evil doers are evil dreaders.

Oghri oghriliqini qilmisa, közige uyqu kelmes.
Without theft, the thief finds no solace in slumber.
Idiomatic Meaning: A leopard never changes its spots.

Oghri tiken yayaqqa heqiqetni chüshendüridu.
Thorn in the foot reveals the truth to the barefoot traveller.
Literal Meaning: The proverb implies that the thorn's pain causes the barefoot man, who may have been unaware of or oblivious to certain truths, to realise or understand them. It signifies that adversity or challenging circumstances can serve as catalysts for gaining insight,

wisdom, or a deeper understanding of the world. In essence, the proverb emphasises that discomfort, adversity, or even painful experiences can lead to personal growth, self-awareness, and a better understanding of reality. It suggests that sometimes, we must face brutal truths to gain a clearer perspective on life.

Oghrining aldida pul - mëlingni maxtima.
Avoid praising your riches in the company of a thief.
Literal Meaning: It advises individuals to exercise caution and discretion when displaying their wealth, possessions, or personal advantages, as this can attract the attention of those with malicious intent. It promotes a sense of prudence, humility, and awareness of one's surroundings to safeguard oneself and one's belongings.

Oghrining ikki yüzi qara.
The face of a thief reveals a duality of darkness.
Idiomatic Meaning: there is honour among thieves.

Oghrining yüriki pok - pok.
The thief's heart quickens its pace.
Idiomatic Meaning: a guilty conscience needs no accuser; there's no peace for the wicked.

Oghul dadisini doraydu, qiz anisini (doraydu)
The son takes after his father, and the daughter takes after his mother.
Idiomatic Meaning: Like father, like son; Like mother, like daughter.

Öküz bolidighan kala, mozay chëghidila belgülik bolidu.
The one destined to be an ox is apparent even in its calfhood. (Kashgari 1072–74)
Literal Meaning: It is important to note that the proverb does not imply that an individual's future success or development is entirely predetermined or fixed. It suggests that specific early indications or qualities can serve as clues to their potential. The proverb reminds us to

be observant and attentive to the early signs of potential in individuals, recognising that some traits or behaviours exhibited during their early stages can indicate their future capabilities or achievements.

Öküzning ayighi bolghiche, mozayning bëshi bolghan yaxshi.
Being a calf's head is better than a cow's hoof. (Kashgari 1072–74)
Literal Meaning: The proverb suggests that it is preferable to be independent, where one can exercise control and make essential choices, rather than being in a subordinate position with limited power or autonomy.

Ölgendin këyin 'yasin' oqughanning nëme paydisi.
Once life has departed, the recitation of Yasin[6] holds no significance.
Idiomatic Meaning: It is no use crying over spilt milk; it is too late to shut the stable door after the horse has bolted; when a thing is done, advice comes too late.

Ölgenning eyibini kolima.
Do not dig into the faults of the dead.
Idiomatic Meaning: Never speak ill of the dead.

Ölgüsi kelgen chashqan, müshükning quyruqigha ësiliptu.
Desiring demise, the mouse snared the cat's tail. (Kashgari 1072–74)
Literal Meaning: The proverb emphasises that such actions can lead to unintended consequences or even worsen the situation, akin to the mouse provoking the cat and potentially facing a more dangerous outcome. It serves as a cautionary reminder against self-destructive tendencies and encourages seeking healthier ways to address challenges and find solutions.

---

[6] One of the Quranic Surahs

Ölmes aghriq chiqmas jan.
   Long-lasting illness has an immortal life.
   Idiomatic Meaning: A creaking door hangs longest.

Ölmigen janda ümid bar.
   If breath remains, hope perseveres.
   Idiomatic Meaning: While there's life, there's hope;
   hope springs eternal.

Ölüktin këpen tileptu, qumluqtin yiken (tileptu)
   One seeks a shroud from the departed and searches for a
   cattail in the desert.
   Idiomatic Meaning: what can you expect from a pig but
   a grunt?.

On gepchidin bir ishchan ela.
   An active doer surpasses ten mere speakers.
   Idiomatic Meaning: Actions speak louder than words;
   fine words, butter, no parsnips.

Ongda yatqan girde yeptu, ketmen chapqan jigde (yeptu)
   The man lying in bed eats bread, while the worker
   nourishes on oleaster.
   Literal Meaning: The proverb "the man lying in bed eats
   bread, while the worker nourishes on oleaster" highlights
   the disparity between two individuals and their
   approaches to sustenance. It signifies that one person,
   represented by the man in bed, enjoys the fruits of
   comfort and convenience without exerting much effort. In
   contrast, the worker, symbolising someone who engages
   in hard work, sustains themselves with the wild and less
   desirable oleaster. The proverb serves as a reminder that
   those who work diligently and persevere tend to reap the
   rewards of their labour, while those who remain idle or
   depend on the efforts of others may only have access to
   introductory provisions. It emphasises the value of
   diligence, self-reliance, and the willingness to seek

sustenance through active engagement rather than relying on the efforts of others.

Öngkür bolsimu öyüm yaxshiken.
Though a cave it may be, my dwelling surpasses grandeur.
Idiomatic Meaning: Home is home, though it's never so homely.

Oqughan oghul atisidin ela.
An educated son surpasses his father.
Idiomatic Meaning: Learning is better than house and land.

Ot bilen oynashma,.
Do not play with fire.
Idiomatic Meaning: do not play with fire.

Ötken ishqa saliwat.
Let the past find its rest.
Idiomatic Meaning: Let bygones be bygones.

Otni yalqun bilen öchürgili bolmas.
A flame cannot extinguish a fire. (Kashgari 1072–74)
Literal Meaning: It suggests a different approach or strategy to address the issue. It encourages finding alternative solutions, seeking understanding, practising nonviolent communication, or using peaceful means to resolve conflicts. The proverb highlights the importance of choosing wise and peaceful approaches to overcome challenges and conflicts to achieve a more positive outcome.

Ottuz yëshida er atalghan, qiriq yëshida shir atilar.
He who is called a man at thirty shall be hailed as a lion by forty.
Idiomatic Meaning: Life begins at forty.

Owchi qanche hile bilse, ëyiqmu shunche yol bilidu.
The more cunning the hunter becomes, the cleverer the
bear adapts. (Kashgari 1072–74)
Literal Meaning: It suggests that individuals or groups
facing challenges or threats may develop their
intelligence, resourcefulness, and strategies to overcome
them. It implies that adversity can lead to developing
skills and abilities that help navigate difficult situations.
The proverb serves as a reminder of the dynamic
relationship between predators and prey and the capacity
of living beings to adapt and respond to the challenges
they encounter in their environment.

Öy igisi bolmisa, öchkining ëti abduraxman.
When the owner fades away, the goat bears the name
Abdulrahman.
Idiomatic Meaning: When the cat's away, the mice will
play.

Öy tutsang balada qalding, tutmisang talada (qalding)
If you marry, trouble may find you; if you do not, you
may wander as a homeless soul.
Idiomatic Meaning: needles and pins, needles and pins,
when a man marries, his trouble begins.

Öydiki hësab bazargha yarimaptu.
The budget at home aligns differently from the market.
Literal Meaning: It highlights the difference between
managing finances within a controlled domestic setting
and dealing with the market's unpredictable and
fluctuating nature or broader economic environment. The
proverb encourages individuals to recognise and navigate
the distinct differences between managing personal
finances and dealing with the complexities of the market,
emphasising the need for flexibility, adaptability, and
informed decision-making in financial matters.

Öyni oghri alghandin këyin ishik taqaptu.
One locks the door after it has been robbed.
Idiomatic Meaning: It is too late to shut the stable door after the horse has bolted.

Öyni öy etken xotun.
Within the embrace of a wife, a house finds its essence.
Literal Meaning: It highlights the importance of a wife or partner in creating and maintaining a harmonious and complete household. It emphasises a wife's essential role in the overall functioning and well-being of a family. The proverb conveys that a wife's role and presence are indispensable in creating a nurturing and thriving home, emphasising the significance of a loving partnership in a family's overall well-being and happiness.

Öyning berikiti xotundin, qazanning berikiti otundin.
The blessing of a house stems from the wife's care, just as the blessing of a pot arises from the wood's contribution.
Idiomatic Meaning: The grey mare is the better horse.

Öz öyümning boshluqi, put - qolumning xoshluqi.
The confines of my own home hold the essence of contentment, where my feet find solace, and my hands find joy.
Idiomatic Meaning: There's no place like home.

Öz putigha özi palta chëpiptu.
He cuts himself with his own axe.
Idiomatic Meaning: beaten with his owne rod.

Özge kishining mali, mal sanalmas.
Count not others' wealth as your own (Kashgari 1072–74)
Literal Meaning: The proverb reminds us to appreciate and make the most of our resources and opportunities rather than constantly comparing ourselves to others and longing for what they have. It encourages self-reliance, self-acceptance, and the cultivation of inner wealth rather

than relying on external validation or material possessions for one's sense of worth and happiness.

Özi chirayliqning qiliqi chirayliq.
A handsome man possesses a beautiful manner.
Idiomatic Meaning: handsome is as handsome does; manners maketh the man.

Özi kolighan origha özi chüshüptu.
He who digs a hole for others finds himself falling into it.
Idiomatic Meaning: as you make your bed, so you must lie on it.

Özi setning qiliqi set.
An ugly man carries an ugly manner.
Idiomatic Meaning: Handsome is as handsome does.

Özi yoqning yüzi yoq.
One who is not present has no face.
Idiomatic Meaning: He who is absent is always in the wrong.

Özini maxtighan ikkinchi axmaq.
It is the mark of a second fool to boast of oneself.
Idiomatic Meaning: self-praise is no recommendation.

Özini sorighan sheher soraptu.
He who can master self-control possesses the capacity to govern a city.
Idiomatic Meaning: Self trust is the first secret of success.

Özüngni bil, özgini qoy.
Know thyself, and leave others be.
Idiomatic Meaning: know thyself; paddle your own canoe; to each, his own.

Özüngni ching tut, xoshnangni oghri tutma.
Be accountable for your own actions and avoid labelling

your neighbour a thief.
Idiomatic Meaning: Good fences make good neighbours.

Özüngni xar qilghuche küchüngni xar qil.
Utilise your strength rather than diminishing yourself.
Idiomatic Meaning: Better to light one's candle than to curse the darkness.

Padishahning emri wajip.
The king's order is an imperative.
Idiomatic Meaning: The king can do no wrong.

Pakizlik imandin kelidu.
Cleanliness comes from faith.
Idiomatic Meaning: cleanliness is next to Godliness.

Paqirghanning hemhisi altun emes.
All that glitters is not gold.
Idiomatic Meaning: all that glitters is not gold.

Patmichuqning kële bolmiqi ming yil.
It takes a thousand years for a gecko to become a komodo dragon.
Idiomatic Meaning: It takes three generations to make a gentleman.

Patqaqtin qutulup, sazliqqa kirip qaptu.
Escaping the mud, he plunged into the swamp.
Idiomatic Meaning: out of the frying pan into the fire.

Paxta ichide ot saqlighili bolmas.
Fire cannot be contained by cotton.
Literal Meaning: The proverb is a cautionary reminder that keeping secrets hidden for an extended period is challenging. It suggests that the truth has a way of emerging or becoming known, and attempts to conceal it are often temporary or futile. It emphasises that secrets are likely to be revealed eventually, just as fire cannot be contained within cotton.

Pezilet tile, öginish bilen meghrurlanma, peziletsiz turup
meghrurlansa, sinaqta hoduqidu.
Seek virtue and pursue knowledge humbly; pride without
integrity crumbles in adversity. (Kashgari 1072–74)
Literal Meaning: The proverb conveys the importance of
cultivating moral character and approaching learning with
humility. It emphasises that true wisdom goes hand in
hand with ethical conduct. While acquiring knowledge is
valuable, it is essential to maintain integrity and not let
pride overshadow one's actions. When faced with difficult
circumstances or tests, individuals who lack integrity and
exhibit arrogance are more likely to falter or fail. The
proverb underscores the significance of combining
intellectual growth with ethical values and humility for
enduring success and resilience in life's trials.

Pichaq bilen oynashma, qol këser.
A hand toying with a knife invites its own wound.
Idiomatic Meaning: Do not play with edged tools.

Pichaq qanche ittik bolsimu, öz sëpini yonuyalmas.
No matter how sharp the knife is, it cannot carve its own
handle. (Kashgari 1072–74)
Literal Meaning: This proverb highlights the inherent
limitation of self-reliance and self-creation. It suggests
that even if one possesses exceptional skills or abilities,
they cannot solely shape their circumstances or create
their support systems. It emphasises the need for
collaboration, interdependence, and seeking assistance
from others when necessary, recognising that certain tasks
or achievements require external assistance that cannot be
accomplished alone.

Pichaqni özüngge sal, aghrimisa kishige (sal)
Stab yourself with a knife first; if it does not hurt, then
stab others.
Idiomatic Meaning: Do as you would be done by. Do
unto others as you would they should do unto you.

Pitning achchiqida chapanni ochaqqa salma!.
Do not scorch the quilt to banish the lice.
Idiomatic Meaning: Don't throw the baby out with the bathwater.

Pul bolsa janggalda shorpa.
Having money allows you to enjoy a delicious soup even in the jungle.
Idiomatic Meaning: Money makes the mare to go.

Puli bar bazargha mangar, puli yoq mazargha (mangar)
The wealthy go to the bazaar, while the poor go to the Mazar(shrine)
Literal Meaning: The proverb reflects the socio-economic divide and individuals' paths based on financial circumstances. It suggests wealthier individuals have more opportunities and resources to focus on material pursuits and economic endeavours. At the same time, those who are economically disadvantaged may rely more on spiritual or religious practices to cope with their challenges and find hope. The proverb serves as a commentary on the differing paths taken by individuals with varying financial means, highlighting the influence of wealth and poverty on the choices and activities of individuals in society.

Pulni pul tapidu.
Money makes money.
Idiomatic Meaning: Money makes money.

Pulning tili yoq.
Money has no language.
Literal Meaning: It emphasises the universal nature of money as a medium of exchange. It suggests that money transcends linguistic and cultural barriers, being universally understood and accepted. Regardless of one's native language or background, money is valuable and can be used for transactions and commerce across

different societies and regions. The proverb underscores money's practical and universal function in facilitating economic transactions and interactions.

Pup tapquche eqil tap.
Earn wisdom before you earn money.
Idiomatic Meaning: A fool and his money are soon parted.

Qagha balam ap'aq balam, kirpe balam yumshaq (balam)
The crow adores her white child, and the hedgehog treasures her soft baby.
Literal Meaning: The poetic language and imagery used in the proverb evoke a sense of tenderness and warmth, emphasising the strong bond between a parent and child in the animal kingdom. It serves as a reminder of the universal nature of parental love, cutting across species and highlighting the innate nurturing instincts in the natural world. This proverb underscores the deep affection and attachment parents have for their children, celebrating the beauty and preciousness of the parent-child relationship and the beauty of parental love, which sees beyond physical appearances and values the essence of each child.

Qagha ghazni dorisa, puti sünar.
When a crow imitates a goose, it risks breaking its foot. (Kashgari 1072–74)
Literal Meaning: The proverb reminds us to embrace our strengths, talents, and individuality rather than striving to imitate others. It encourages self-awareness, authenticity, and being true to ourselves. It advises against pursuing paths not meant for us and reminds us to appreciate and make the most of our unique qualities and capabilities. The proverb warns against the perils of imitation without considering one's limitations, urging individuals to stay true to themselves and not attempt to be something they are not.

Qagha qaghining közini choqimaydu.
A crow does not peck another crow's eye.
Idiomatic Meaning: Hawks will not pick out hawks'
eyes.

Qaghining qërisini kim biler, kishining alisini kim tapar.
Who knows a crow's age, and who can unravel the
wickedness within a man? (Kashgari 1072–74)
Literal Meaning: It suggests that judging a person's
character or true nature is far more complex and
challenging than determining the age of a crow. It
highlights the idea that one cannot accurately gauge an
individual's moral or ethical qualities based solely on
superficial observations or limited information. It
encourages individuals to approach others with a sense of
understanding, empathy, and an awareness that true
understanding of a person's character requires deeper
insight and genuine connection.

Qanni qan bilen yughili bolmas.
Blood cannot cleanse the blood (Kashgari 1072–74)
Literal Meaning: It expresses that violence, wrongdoing,
or harm cannot be rectified or undone by further violence
or harm. It suggests that seeking revenge or justice
through violent means only perpetuates a cycle of
violence and does not bring about proper resolution or
healing. The proverb serves as a reminder that responding
to harm or injustice with more harm does not lead to
positive outcomes, and it encourages individuals to seek
peaceful resolutions and reconciliation instead.

Qara bulutni yel achar, hökümet ishikini para achar.
The wind disperses black clouds, while the bribe opens
the doors of government. (Kashgari 1072–74)
Literal Meaning: The proverb highlights two different
scenarios. The first part, " the wind disperses black
clouds," symbolises the idea that challenging times will
eventually pass. Just as the wind disperses dark clouds,

indicating the end of a storm, this proverb suggests that hardships and troubles will eventually fade away or be resolved. It reflects optimism and the belief that tough times are temporary. The second part, " while bribe opens the doors of government" refers to the corrupt practice of using bribes or unethical means to gain access or influence in governmental or authoritative circles. It implies that in some cases, bribery or offering monetary incentives can help bypass obstacles or gain favoritism within government institutions. However, it should be noted that this proverb does not endorse or promote bribery but rather acknowledges its existence as a negative aspect of certain systems or societies.

Qarighugha këche - kündüzning perqi yoq.
In the blind's world, day and night share no sight.
Idiomatic Meaning: A blind man's wife needs no paint.

Qarighuning yurtigha barsang bir közüngni qisiwal.
If you go to the land of the blind, close one eye.
Idiomatic Meaning: When in Rome, do as the Romans do.

Qawighan It chishlimeydu, chishleydighan It maraydu.
A dog that barks does not bite, but a dog that bites may lurk in shadows.
Idiomatic Meaning: A barking dog never bites; barking dogs seldom bite.

Qazagha riza, balagha sewri.
Embrace the calamity, and with patience, endure the disaster.
Idiomatic Meaning: bear and forbear.

Qazi ach qalsa bazar këzidu, sopi ach qalsa mazar (këzidu)
When the qadi[7] is hungry, he goes to the bazaar; when the Sufi is hungry, he turns to the *Mazar*. (graveyard)

---

[7] judge

Literal Meaning: "This proverb draws a parallel between the actions of the *qadi* (a judge) and the *Sufi* (a seeker of wisdom or knowledge). It suggests that individuals with different roles or inclinations pursue nourishment or fulfilment in distinct ways. The proverb highlights that when the *qadi*, representing a figure involved in legal matters and worldly affairs, experiences hunger, they seek sustenance in the market. This reflects a practical and pragmatic approach, focusing on meeting their basic needs within the material realm. On the other hand, when the sopi, symbolising someone on a quest for wisdom or spiritual enlightenment, feel hunger, they seek solace at the *mazar* (a sacred place associated with spirituality or the resting place of a revered figure). This signifies their inclination to nourish their inner self, seeking fulfilment through spiritual practices, introspection, or connecting with higher realms of consciousness. In essence, the proverb underscores the idea that different individuals, based on their roles, aspirations, or inner inclinations, will seek nourishment or solace in ways that align with their respective paths. It recognises the diversity of human experiences and the varied approaches people adopt to satisfy and fulfil their needs.

Qëlin muz bir künde muzlimaydu.

Thick ice does not freeze overnight.
Idiomatic Meaning: Rome was not built in a day.

Qëri öküz paltidin qorqmas.

The old ox fears not the axe's presence. (Kashgari 1072–74)
Literal Meaning: The proverb suggests that with age and a deep understanding of life's transience, the old ox has transcended the fear of death. Having witnessed the passage of time and accepting the cycle of life and death, it has attained a sense of inner peace and serenity. By connecting the absence of fear towards both mortality and the presence of the axe, this proverb conveys a profound

message about embracing the impermanence of life and facing challenges without trepidation. It symbolises wisdom and acceptance, emphasising the courage and fearlessness that can be achieved through a deep understanding of life's inevitable truths.

Qëri qushqach këpekke aldanmas.

The old bird cannot be fooled by the miller's bran.
Idiomatic Meaning: You cannot catch old birds with chaff.

Qërilar sözi bikar ketmes.

Elderly people's words were said not in vain. (Kashgari 1072–74)
Literal Meaning: In Uyghur cultures, older individuals are respected for their wisdom and are considered sources of guidance and advice. Their words are often seen as valuable contributions based on their years of experience and observation. This proverb serves as a reminder to listen attentively and respect the wisdom shared by older generations. It encourages us to recognise the wisdom that comes with age and to appreciate the valuable insights and lessons that can be gained from the experiences of those who have lived longer. It is a reminder to value and honour the wisdom and knowledge passed down from older generations, recognising that their words often hold great meaning and significance.

Qeshqerning[8] qish az, soghuqi etiyaz.

Kashgar's winter is brief, but its spring is a chilly

---

[8] Kashgar, located at the Taklamakan Desert's edge and in the Tarim Basin's far western reaches, is a city steeped in history. Its position in the Uygur Region, a remote oasis city with a diverse population, adds to its historical significance. The predominantly Uyghur city uniquely blends desert landscapes, mountain ranges, and cultural diversity. Geographically, Kashgar is positioned between the Taklamakan Desert to the east and the Tengri Tagh Mountain Range to the north. To the west, beyond the Pamir Mountains, lies Tajikistan, Afghanistan and Pakistan. Historically, the city's location has made it an important trading hub along

embrace.

Literal Meaning: This proverb describes the climatic characteristics of Kashgar, a region known for having a brief winter and a cold spring. It suggests that the winter season in Kashgar is short-lived, indicating that the harsh cold and severe weather conditions associated with winter are relatively brief. However, it also notes that the arrival of spring in Kashgar brings a lingering chill, indicating that even during the transition into the warmer season, the temperatures remain cool. This proverb serves as a reminder that the weather patterns in certain regions can be unique and distinctive, with specific characteristics that deviate from the norm. It captures the essence of Kashgar's climate, highlighting the peculiarities of its winter and spring seasons. In essence, this proverb draws attention to the climate of Kashgar, showcasing the transient nature of its winter and the persistent chill of its spring. It serves as a reminder of the diversity and variety found in different regions and the importance of understanding and adapting to the unique characteristics of each place.

Idiomatic Meaning: March comes in like a lion and goes out like a lamb.

Qëtiq ichken qutuldi, ayaq yalighan tutuldi.

The one who sipped the yoghurt escaped, while the one who licked it faced capture.

Idiomatic Meaning: Little thieves are hanged, but great ones escape.

Qilalsang qil, bolmisa boldi qil.

Do it if you can, or gracefully let it go if you cannot.

Idiomatic Meaning: shit or get off the pot.

---

the Silk Road, connecting China with Central Asia and the Middle East, enlightening us about its past glory.

Qildek semimiyetlik, pildek ataqtin ela.
A small act of honesty outweighs the weight of a colossal ill-repute.
Idiomatic Meaning: he that has an ill name is half hanged; a hungry man is an angry man.

Qildin ketseng qiriqtin kётisen.
One false stitch unravels forty threads.
Idiomatic Meaning: A miss is as good as a mile.

Qilich qёnida tursa dat basidu.
If a sword remains in its sheath, it will gather rust.
Idiomatic Meaning: Use it or lose it.

Qilichning küchidin, qelemning küchi artuq.
The might of the pen triumphs over the might of the sword.
Idiomatic Meaning: The pen is mightier than the sword.

Qirdiki qirghawulni owlaymen dep, öydiki toxuni qoldin chiqirip qoyma.
Do not sacrifice the chicken in your coop for the elusive pheasant in the field. (Kashgari 1072–74)
Literal Meaning: It advises against neglecting or disregarding something valuable within reach to pursue something more desirable but potentially elusive. The proverb serves as a reminder to appreciate and cherish the present, not to be blinded by the allure of external desires, and to focus on nurturing and safeguarding what is already in one's possession. It encourages a balanced approach that values both immediate benefits and long-term aspirations.

Qish közi qarighu.
Winter is blind.
Literal Meaning: The proverb suggests that people can dress however they want during the cold season without being judged or criticised for their fashion choices. It implies that winter weather conditions, such as low

temperatures and the need for warmth, override societal expectations or norms regarding clothing and style. In many cultures, winter is associated with bundling up in layers of clothing to stay warm and protect oneself from the cold. The proverb emphasises that individuals can prioritise their comfort and practicality over adhering to fashion trends or social appearance standards during this time. It implies that the focus shifts from outward appearances to personal well-being and the need for insulation against the elements. It encourages individuality and self-expression, allowing people to wear what makes them feel comfortable and protected, regardless of whether it aligns with prevailing fashion trends or conventional aesthetics. However, it is important to note that the proverb should not be interpreted as advocating for disregarding appropriate attire or neglecting personal grooming. Instead, it emphasises the freedom to prioritise warmth and practicality over external appearances during winter.

Qiz bilen chëlishma, baytal bilen chëpishma.

Do not engage in battle with a maiden nor race against a spirited mare. (Kashgari 1072–74)
Idiomatic Meaning: The grey mare is the better horse; the female of the species is more deadly than the male.

Qizim sanga eytay, kelinim sen angla.

I speak to my daughter, trusting my daughter-in-law will listen.
Literal Meaning: It is an example of diverted speech or indirect communication. It is a way of conveying a message or expressing a request indirectly by addressing one person while intending the message for someone else. In this case, the speaker addresses their daughter but intends for the daughter-in-law to understand the message or expectation. This form of communication can be used in various situations to convey messages discreetly or to avoid confrontation.

Qoghun tallansa, igisimu ikki qoli bilen tallar.
When choosing a melon, the owner picks it with both
hands. (Kashgari 1072–74)
Literal Meaning: The proverb implies that when
someone takes possession or ownership of something
valuable, they should do so with care and responsibility.
The melon represents something valuable, and picking it
with both hands suggests a level of attentiveness and
appreciation for its worth. The proverb emphasises the
importance of treating valuable possessions or
opportunities respectfully and trying to handle them
properly. It can be interpreted as a reminder to show
gratitude and take responsibility when entrusted with
something valuable.

Qol qolini yusa, qol yüzni yuyar.
One hand washes the other, and together, they wash the
face.
Idiomatic Meaning: One hand washes the other; you
scratch my back, I'll scratch yours; if every man would
sweep his own doorstep, the city would soon be clean.

Qongamda ishtan yoq ëtim marjan büwi.
I may lack the attire, but my name is Baroness.
Literal Meaning: It implies that even though someone
may not possess material wealth or possessions, they still
try to boast and appear affluent by associating themselves
with expensive or luxurious things.

Qorqqan awwal mush kötürer.
The timid heart is quick to fight.
Idiomatic Meaning: the weakest go to the wall.

Qorqqan kishige qoy bëshi qosh körüner.
A frightened man sees a sheep's head as double. (Kashgari
1072–74)
Literal Meaning: When someone is in a state of fear or
panic, they may perceive ordinary things as much more

threatening or alarming than they are. This highlights how fear can distort perception and make even harmless things seem intimidating or overwhelming.

Qorqqanni ejel qoghlar.
Death pursues the frightened.
Idiomatic Meaning: Courage lost, all lost.

Qorqunchaq ölmey turup ming qëtim öler.
A coward dies a thousand times without dying.
Idiomatic Meaning: Cowards die many times before their death. The valiant never taste death but once.

Qorsiqi achning achchiqi yaman.
A hungry man is an angry man.
Idiomatic Meaning: A hungry man is an angry man.

Qosh qilich bir qin'gha sighmas.
Two swords cannot fit in one sheath. (Kashgari 1072–74)
Literal Meaning: It denotes that two conflicting or incompatible things or people cannot coexist harmoniously in the same situation or relationship. It suggests that when two opposing forces or individuals exist, it is difficult for them to coexist peacefully or successfully without conflict or competition. Just as two swords cannot be stored together in one sheath without causing damage, it implies that certain situations require separation or resolution of conflicts for peaceful coexistence.

Qoshnamning qosh körüner.
The Neighbour's possession seems twice as grand.
Idiomatic Meaning: the grass is always greener on the other side of the fence.

Qoy özining pëyide ësilidu, adem öz gunahini tartidu.
Where the sheep meets its stake, the man fully confronts his sins.

Idiomatic Meaning: Every tub must stand on its own bottom.

Qulan padisi yol bashlighuchisiz bolmas.
Horses herd cannot be without a guide. (Kashgari 1072–74)
Literal Meaning: It emphasises the need for leadership and direction in any group or organisation. It suggests that a group of horses, or any collective entity, requires a knowledgeable and capable guide to ensure order, direction, and cohesion. The herd may become disorganised or lose its way without a guide or leader. The proverb serves as a reminder of the significance of effective leadership and its role in maintaining unity and achieving collective goals.

Qulaq bilen anglighan yalghan, köz bilen körgen rast.
What you hear lies, and what you see is the truth.
Idiomatic Meaning: Believe nothing of what you hear, and only half of what you see.

Qum yighilsa tagh bolur.
With each grain amassed, sand transforms into a mountain.
Idiomatic Meaning: Take care of the pence, and the pounds will take care of themselves.

Quruq chëlek taraqlaydu, nadan walaqlaydu.
Empty buckets sound aloud, the ignorant roars.
Idiomatic Meaning: Empty vessels make the most sound.

Quruq gep ishekke yük.
Nonsense weighs heavy, burdening even the humblest donkey.
Literal Meaning: It highlights the universal nature of the negative impact of nonsense, emphasising that even someone or something perceived as patient or uncomplaining (like a donkey) would find it burdensome.

It serves as a reminder that engaging in or tolerating nonsensical behaviour is generally considered unpleasant or problematic.

Quruq gepke müshükmu aptapqa chiqmaydu.
Where there are no fish, there shall be no cat.
Idiomatic Meaning: Nothing comes of nothing.

Quruq geptin kachat yaxshi.
A slap is better than an empty promise.
Literal Meaning: Actions carry more weight and value than mere words. It emphasises the importance of reliability, honesty, and keeping one's commitments. It suggests that someone should take action, even if it involves a negative consequence like a slap, rather than making promises they cannot or will not fulfil. It is worth noting that this proverb is metaphorical and should not be taken literally. It serves as a reminder that trust and actions speak louder than empty words or broken promises.

Quruq qoshuq ëghizgha yarimas, quruq söz qulaqqa.
Just as an empty spoon cannot satisfy the mouth's plea, an empty promise fails to appease attentive ears. (Kashgari 1072–74)
Literal Meaning: It highlights the importance of substance and reliability. Just as an empty spoon cannot provide nourishment, an empty promise fails to fulfil its intended purpose of creating trust, assurance, or delivering on commitments. It implies that actions, honesty, and a sincere desire to follow through should support promises. By employing this proverb serves as a reminder that people value tangible results and genuine intentions rather than empty words or promises without substance.

Quruq/bosh taghar öre turmaydu.
An empty sack does not stand upright.

Idiomatic Meaning: Empty sacks will never stand upright.

Qush qaniti bilen, er ëti bilen.
As a bird soars with its wings, a man finds strength alongside his horse. (Kashgari 1072–74)
Literal Meaning: Birds are designed for flight, and their wings are crucial for moving freely in their natural element, the sky. It suggests that a bird without its wings would be incomplete or unable to realize its potential fully. The proverb suggests that a man finds his greatest fulfilment and purpose when he has a horse. Horses have played an integral role in human (Uyghur) history, serving as loyal companions, partners in labour, and aids in transportation. The presence of a horse provides a sense of connection, strength, and harmony with nature for a man. The proverb conveys the notion that creatures thrive and are at their best when they possess the qualities or relationships that are inherent to their nature. It underscores the significance of embracing and nurturing the aspects that bring about the greatest fulfilment and enable individuals to reach their highest potential.

Qush tuzaqqa yem üchün iliner.
Bird finds its trap in the lure of bait. (Kashgari 1072–74)
Literal Meaning: metaphorically, it encourages individuals to be aware of traps or schemes that might lead them into undesirable situations or harm. It underscores the importance of being mindful, cautious, and discerning in making decisions and avoiding pitfalls.

Qushqachtin qorqqan tëriq tërimaptu.
One who fears the birds cannot sow the flaxseed.
Idiomatic Meaning: If you don't like the heat, get out of the kitchen.

Qut belgüsi bilik.
Knowledge is a sign of happiness. (Kashgari 1072–74)

Literal Meaning: The proverb "knowledge is a sign of happiness" suggests that knowing can contribute to a person's happiness. Knowledge can lead to personal growth, confidence, and a sense of achievement, all of which enhance overall well-being. While it is not the only factor in happiness, knowledge plays a significant role in creating a fulfilling life.

Qutadghu bilik.

Knowledge brings happiness.
See: qut belgüsi bilik. Kashgari –.
Literal Meaning: Knowledge has the potential to bring happiness. By acquiring knowledge, we expand our understanding, gain new perspectives, and develop skills that can contribute to personal growth and fulfilment. Knowledge empowers us to make informed decisions, pursue our passions, and navigate the complexities of life with greater confidence. It opens doors to opportunities, fosters personal development, and broadens our horizons. Through the pursuit and application of knowledge, we can experience a sense of accomplishment, satisfaction, and joy.

Quyash tangni yorutar, kitab angni yorutar.

Where the sun illuminates the dawn, books awaken the conscience.
Literal Meaning: It symbolises the importance of natural and intellectual enlightenment sources. The sun represents the natural world and its ability to bring light and new beginnings. In contrast, books represent human knowledge and wisdom, awakening our conscience and expanding our understanding of the world.

Quyruqini kötürgen kala chichmay qalmaptu.

An elevated tail of a cow foretells the presence of dung.
Idiomatic Meaning: If anything can go wrong, it will.

Saghlam tende saghlam eqil.
A sound mind in a sound body.
Idiomatic Meaning: sound mind, sound body.

Samanning tëgidin su quyuptu.
Allowing water to flow under wheat hay.
Literal Meaning: The proverb emphasises the deliberate and strategic nature of not informing or disclosing one's activities. It suggests that the individual is intentionally keeping their actions concealed, allowing their plan or strategy to progress without the knowledge or interference of others.

Sanga bëqip men, ishikke bëqip dem.
As the door's size determines its lock, your behaviour reflects mine in stock.
Idiomatic Meaning: The door swings both ways; circumstances alter cases.

Sap hawa, ten'ge dawa.
Fresh air is a cure for the body.
Literal Meaning: It highlights the importance of clean, fresh air in promoting physical health and well-being. It underscores the positive impact that being in environments with good air quality can have on various aspects of the body's functioning and recovery processes.

Seher qopqan sa'adet, waqche qopqan palaket.
Rising early brings grace while waking late leads to a clumsy pace.
Idiomatic Meaning: The early bird catches the worm; early to bed and early to rise make a man healthy, wealthy, and wise.

Sewri qilghan muradigha yëter.
Patience paves the path to one's goal.
Idiomatic Meaning: He with patience can have what he will; all things come to those who wait; good things come to those who wait.

Sewri qilsang ghoridin halwa pishar.
Through patience, the green apricot ripens to sweet
fruition.
Idiomatic Meaning: All things come to those who wait;
good things come to those who wait.

Sewrning tëgi altun.
Patience is gold.
Idiomatic Meaning: Patience is a virtue.

Shamal chiqmisa derex lingshimas.
If the wind doesn't blow, the tree stays still.
Idiomatic Meaning: No smoke without fire; there is no
smoke without fire.

*Shirin sözliseng, yilan indin chiqar, achchiq sözliseng
musulman dindin (chiqar)*
Sweet words coax the snake from its nest, while bitter
words may turn even a Muslim atheist.
Idiomatic Meaning: with a sweet tongue and kindness,
you can drag an elephant by a hair.

Sodigerning ozuqi ërigh bolsa, yol üstide yer.
He confidently dines on the road when the merchant's
earnings are clean. (Kashgari 1072–74)
Literal Meaning: The proverb conveys that when a
person's wealth or earnings are acquired through
legitimate and upright means, they can confidently enjoy
the rewards publicly and unreservedly. It highlights the
importance of ethical conduct and integrity in business or
personal endeavours, as clean earnings bring a sense of
satisfaction and allow for open enjoyment without fear of
judgment or negative consequences. This proverb
emphasises the value of earning wealth or success through
honest means, suggesting that it enables individuals to
openly enjoy the benefits of their labour without
hesitation or guilt. It promotes the idea that ethical
conduct and integrity in earning are essential for personal

well-being and society's acceptance of one's
achievements.

Sözge mezze qilsa, tutqun bolur.
Entrapped by the allure of sweet words, man becomes a
captive. (Kashgari 1072–74)
Literal Meaning: The proverb warns against blindly
accepting or enjoying sweet or flattering words, as it can
lead to a loss of personal freedom or falling under the
control of others. It urges individuals to remain vigilant
and discerning when encountering persuasive language or
insincere praise.

Su ichken quduqqa tükürme.
Do not spit at the well from which you have quenched
your thirst.
Literal Meaning: The proverb highlights the importance
of appreciating and showing gratitude to the things or
individuals that have contributed positively to your life. It
serves as a reminder to be mindful of the benefits or
support you have received and to avoid disparaging or
disrespecting those sources. It emphasises the value of
gratitude, respect and recognising the positive influences
in one's life, urging individuals to show appreciation
rather than contempt or ingratitude.

Suni körmey ötük salma.
Do not remove your boots until the waters are in sight.
(Kashgari 1072–74)
Idiomatic Meaning: Don't halloo till you are out of the
wood; don't sell the skin till you have caught the bear.

Süt bilen kirgen xuy jan bilen chiqar.
The habit entered with the first feeding and departed with
life's leaving.
Idiomatic Meaning: What's bred in the bone will come
out in the flesh.

Süt ichip aghzi köygen qëtiqnimu püwlep icher.
> The one, once burnt by milk, blows on yoghurt to cool.
> **Idiomatic Meaning:** A burnt child dreads the fire; Once bitten, twice shy.

Tagh taghqa qowushmas, adem ademge qowushur.
> Mountains stand apart, but man connects heart to heart. (Kashgari 1072–74)
> **Literal Meaning:** The proverb conveys that human connections and unity are products of human actions and intentions, in contrast to the static and unchanging nature of natural formations like mountains. It underscores the significance of human agency and the potential for individuals to come together, cooperate, and build meaningful relationships.

Taghda yolwas bolmisa, maymun padishah bolur.
> The monkey claims the throne's height when the mountain lacks a tiger's might.
> **Idiomatic Meaning:** When the cat's away, the mice will play.

Tama - tama köl bolar.
> Drops make a lake.
> **Idiomatic Meaning:** Little strokes fell great oaks; many a little makes a mickle.

Tamche su tashni tësher.
> Drops of water pierce a stone.
> **Idiomatic Meaning:** constant dropping wears away a stone.

Tar yerde ash yëgüche, keng yerde musht ye.
> It is better to be beaten in a broad place than to eat in a cramped place. (Better deserted than crowded.)
> **Literal Meaning:** The proverb emphasises the preference for facing challenges or experiencing difficulties in an open and spacious environment rather than enduring discomfort or constraints in a confined space. It

underscores the importance of freedom, growth, and the ability to recover in unfavourable circumstances.

Tashmu chüshken yerde ëziz.
Stone is valued most in its own home.
Literal Meaning: It emphasises that a stone holds its highest value or preciousness when it is in its home, where it naturally belongs. It encourages us to honour and appreciate the inherent worth of things when they are in their rightful and harmonious environments.

Tashni chaynighili bolmisa, söyüsh kërek.
If you cannot chew a stone, you must kiss it instead. (Kashgari 1072–74)
Idiomatic Meaning: What can't be cured must be endured; if the mountain won't come to Mohammed, then Mohammed must go to the mountain.

Tayghanning yügürükini tülke söymes.
Fox does not admire the swiftness of a hound. (Kashgari 1072–74)
Literal Meaning: Metaphorically, this proverb can be applied to various aspects of life. It highlights how individuals may not value or admire skills, characteristics, or approaches that differ from their own. It underscores the tendency for people to prefer or appreciate qualities that align with their strengths or preferences. The proverb suggests that individuals may not appreciate or admire qualities or abilities that differ significantly from their own. It serves as a reminder to be mindful of our biases and to recognise the value of diverse perspectives and strengths.

Tazning eqli chüshtin këyin.
Bald's wisdom appears in the afternoon.
Idiomatic Meaning: It is easy to be wise after the event.

Tazning kelidighan yëri bökchining dukini.
The hat shop is where the bald finds its remedy. (Kashgari

1072–74)
Literal Meaning: It suggests that a hat shop serves as a destination or solution for individuals who are bald or in need of head coverings. It emphasises that people naturally turn to specialised establishments to fulfil their needs or address their challenges.

Teleylikke qosh këler.
Luck doubles its favour upon the lucky. (Kashgari 1072–74)
Literal Meaning: It suggests that individuals already seen as lucky have an increased chance of encountering further positive outcomes or experiences. It highlights the idea that luck tends to favour those who are already fortunate.

Ten saqliq - zor bayliq.
Health is a great wealth.
Idiomatic Meaning: Health is wealth.

Teqdirge ten ber.
Accept destiny.
Idiomatic Meaning: What can't be cured must be endured.

Tërek miwisi bilen qimmiet.
The value of a tree lies in its fruit.
Literal Meaning: It emphasises that the true worth or value of a tree or any other entity is determined by the quality and nature of the outcomes or results it produces. It underscores the importance of the tangible manifestations of one's actions or existence as a measure of value or significance.

Tëriqni dep tawuzdin ayrilip qaptu.
He lost the watermelon to flaxseed.
Idiomatic Meaning: Do not cut off your nose to spite your face.

Tëriqning bolushi kökidin melum.
The harvest of flaxseed is recognised by its stalk.
Literal Meaning: It suggests that the quality or outcome of a flaxseed harvest can be determined by observing the characteristics or condition of the flax plant itself. It underscores the importance of understanding the underlying factors contributing to a desirable outcome in any endeavour.

Teswining yipi bolidu, her ishning ëpi (bolidu)
Tasbih[9] has a thread, and every problem possesses a solution.
Idiomatic Meaning: every bullet has its billet.

Tewekkül tash yaridu.
Adventure can split the stone.
Idiomatic Meaning: Adventures are to the adventurous.

Teyyar tursang apet körmeysen.
With preparedness, disaster is averted.
Idiomatic Meaning: forewarned is forearmed.

Tëz püküp yashighuche, tik turup ölgen yaxshi.
It is better to die standing up than to live kneeling.
Idiomatic Meaning: It is better to die on your feet than live on your knees; it is better to die on one's feet than live on one's knees.

Tigh yarisi këter, til yarisi ketmes.
A wound from a sword may heal, but a wound from the tongue cannot.
Idiomatic Meaning: A blow with a word strikes deeper than a blow with a sword.

Tikmigüche ünmes, tilimigüche tëpilmas.
It does not grow unless you plant it and cannot be discovered until you try. (Kashgari 1072–74)

---

[9] Prayer Beads

Literal Meaning: Metaphorically, this proverb can be applied to various aspects of life. It emphasises the importance of proactive engagement and active pursuit to experience growth, success, or the realisation of goals. It suggests that valuable or significant outcomes are not obtained passively but through deliberate action and seeking. It suggests that growth and valuable outcomes require intentional effort and active pursuit. It underscores the idea that things develop and become apparent once they are set in motion and actively sought after.

Tili yaman erdin, yalghuz tulluq yaxshi.
Lonely widowhood is preferable to the company of a man with an evil tongue. (Kashgari 1072–74)
Literal Meaning: It suggests that being alone, even in a state of widowhood, is preferable to being in the presence of someone who consistently uses their words to cause harm or spread negativity. It underscores the importance of choosing companions wisely and prioritising a positive and peaceful environment.

Tiliseng taparsen, tërisang orarsen.
What you pray for, you might get; if you sow, you shall reap.
Idiomatic Meaning: he that follows frets, frets will follow him; be careful what you pray for, you might get it.

Töge chong bolghini bilen, mayiqi chong emes.
Though the camel is large, its dung is small. (Kashgari 1072–74)
Literal Meaning: The proverb suggests that the size or appearance of something does not necessarily reflect its impact or consequences. It highlights the need to look beyond superficial aspects and consider the potential significance or effects of seemingly small or inconspicuous elements.

Töge minip qoy arisigha yoshurunalmas.
A camel rider cannot hide among sheep. (Kashgari 1072–74)
Literal Meaning: It suggests that individuals who possess remarkable qualities or stand out from the crowd cannot easily hide or blend in when surrounded by a group lacking those attributes. It underscores the importance of embracing one's uniqueness and authenticity rather than attempting to conform to societal expectations.

Töge oghrilighanmu oghri, tügme oghrilighanmu oghri.
He who steals a camel is a thief, and he who steals a button is still a thief.
Idiomatic Meaning: It is a sin to steal a pin.

Töge qanche bolsa yёghiri shunche.
The larger the camel, the greater the wound.
Idiomatic Meaning: The bigger they are, the harder they fall; big fleas have little fleas upon their backs to bite them, and little fleas have lesser fleas, and so ad infinitum.

Toghra söz qilichtin ötkür.
A right word is sharper than a sword.
Idiomatic Meaning: The pen is mightier than the sword.

Toghra söz tashni yarar, egri söz bashni (yarar)
A right word can split a stone, but a crooked word can break a head.
Idiomatic Meaning: Honey catches more flies than vinegar; a soft answer turneth away wrath.

Tola sözligen tutular, az sözligen qutular.
Excessive talk leads to trouble, while silence offers safety.
Idiomatic Meaning: least said, soonest mended.

Tolun ay qol bilen körsitilmes.
The full moon needs no manual indication. (Kashgari

1072–74)

Literal Meaning: It suggests that the presence of a full moon is unmistakable and does not require manual indication. It highlights that some things in life are prominent and easily recognisable without explicit notification or instruction.

Tömürni qiziqida soq.
Strike while the iron is hot.
Idiomatic Meaning: make hay while the sun shines; strike while the iron is hot.

Tonush emes kishidin, tonush sheytan yaxshi.
A familiar devil is better than a stranger. (Kashgari 1072–74)
Literal Meaning: This proverb highlights that dealing with a known problem or challenge can be wiser, even unpleasant, rather than venturing into uncharted territory with unknown risks and uncertainties. It encourages people to prioritise familiarity and understanding when faced with difficult choices or situations.

Tonush yaghachning putiqi köp.
A familiar tree bears many twigs.
Idiomatic Meaning: Familiarity breeds contempt.

Toshqandek ming yil yashighuche, yolwastek bir kün yasha.
Living a day like a tiger is better than living a thousand years like a rabbit.
Idiomatic Meaning: Better to live one day as a tiger than a thousand years as a sheep.

Töshük marjan yerde qalmas.
A perforated bead will not be left in vain (Kashgari 1072–74)
Literal Meaning: It underscores the notion that valuable items, whether tangible or intangible, tend to attract attention and find their place in various contexts. It encourages recognising the value and importance of

practical things and ensuring they are correctly utilised rather than being left unused or disregarded.

Töt tamning quli.
Servant of the four walls.
Idiomatic Meaning: I'm stuck between the four walls of burdens.

Töwe gunahni yer, sediqe balani.
Regret diminishes sin; charity lessens misfortune.
Idiomatic Meaning: Charity covers a multitude of sins; confession is good for the soul.

Toxu danggal chüsheptu, öchke janggal (chüsheptu)
The hen dreams of muck, while the goat dreams of the jungle.
Idiomatic Meaning: He that drinks beer, thinks beer.

Tughulmighan mozaygha oqur saptu.
Make a trough for an unborn calf.
Idiomatic Meaning: Do not make clothes for a not yet born baby.

Tügmende tughulghan chashqan, hawaning güldürliginidin qorqmas.
A rat born in a mill is not afraid of thunders. (Kashgari 1072–74)
Literal Meaning: It implies that individuals who grow up or live in a specific environment become accustomed to it and are less affected by potential dangers or threats associated with that environment. It underscores the idea that familiarity breeds indifference or fearlessness in the face of adversity.

Tügmini dep tögidin quruq qaptu.
A camel is lost for want of a button.
Idiomatic Meaning: A kingdom is lost for want of a shoe.

Tügminingge özüng barghining yaxshi, gëpingni özüng qilghining yaxshi.
It is better to go to the mill and speak your words.
Idiomatic Meaning: If you would be well served, serve yourself.

Tülke öz inige ürse, qotur bolar.
When a fox attacks its brother, it becomes rabid.
(Kashgari 1072–74)
Literal Meaning: The proverb warns against harming or acting maliciously towards one's kind, which can lead to negative consequences. It emphasises the significance of maintaining unity, cooperation, and treating others with kindness and respect to avoid destructive outcomes.

Tütünning derdini mora bilidu.
The chimney knows the bitterness of the smoke.
Literal Meaning: The proverb emphasises that those directly affected by or involved in a situation have a deeper understanding of its challenges or hardships. It highlights the importance of considering the perspectives of those who have experienced difficulties first-hand and fostering empathy towards their experiences.

Tuxumni tashqa urma.
Do not hit the egg on the stone.
Idiomatic Meaning: Do not spoil the ship for a ha'porth of tar.

Üch qëtim öy köchseng , bir oghlaghliq öchkige ziyan.
Moving home three times is as bad as losing a goat and its kid.
Literal Meaning: It underscores the challenges and disruptions associated with frequent relocations. It likens the negative impact of multiple moves to the loss of a valuable possession, highlighting the importance of stability and a sense of belonging in our lives.

Ulughni ulughlisa qut bolur.

If one honours the great, one will be blessed. (Kashgari 1072–74)

Literal Meaning: It encourages us to acknowledge and uplift the greatness in others, whether it be their accomplishments, talents, or virtues. By doing so, we cultivate a spirit of gratitude and admiration that benefits the individuals being praised and contributes to our personal growth and well-being. It highlights the importance of respecting and admiring those who possess greatness. It suggests that by recognising and honouring the achievements and virtues of others, we invite positive outcomes and blessings into our own lives.

Undaq qazan'gha mundaq chömüch,.

Match the right ladle to the right pot, tit for tat.

Idiomatic Meaning: Ask a silly question, and you get a silly answer; the door swings both ways.   .

Uprighan ya qëpidin, mezmut ya chiqidu.

Old quiver provides a strong arrow. (Kashgari 1072–74)

Literal Meaning: It suggests that the knowledge, skills, and insights gained through years of experience can enhance one's abilities and make one more effective in various endeavours. It emphasises the importance of valuing and learning from the wisdom of older generations and recognising the strength that comes from accumulated knowledge and life experiences. It underscores the significance of experience, wisdom, and knowledge gained over time. It implies that the strength and effectiveness of an individual can be enhanced by drawing upon the lessons and insights acquired through age and accumulated experiences.

Üskek uygha tengri münggüz bermes.

God forbid giving horns to a bad-tempered ox. (Kashgari 1072–74)

Literal Meaning: It underscores the need to prevent or

mitigate the potential harm caused by a bad-tempered or
aggressive entity. It serves as a cautionary statement,
highlighting the importance of restraining or limiting
those who may misuse their abilities or traits to the
detriment of others.

Üzümni ye, sapiqini sorima.
> Eat the grapes, ask not the brunch.
> **Idiomatic Meaning:** Never look a gift horse in the
> mouth.

WaqIt atqan oq.
> Time is a shot.
> **Idiomatic Meaning:** Time flies.

Waqt aldirangghu, saqlap turmaydu.
> Time is impatient and does not wait for any.
> **Idiomatic Meaning:** Time and tide wait for none.

Waqtida bergen nan ölükke kirgen jan.
> A naan in time saves nine.
> **Idiomatic Meaning:** A stitch in time saves nine.

Waqting ketti - bexting ketti.
> Once your time has passed, so too has your happiness.
> **Literal Meaning: It** underscores the significance of
> effectively and consciously utilising our time to enhance
> our happiness and well-being. Making choices that align
> with our values and bring us fulfilment can contribute to a
> more satisfying and meaningful life.

**With diligent preparation during ploughing, harvest
brings unity, not quarrelling.**
> *Sapan waqtida puxtiliq bolsa, xaman waqtida jangjal
> bolmas.* (Kashgari 1072–74)
> **Literal Meaning:** The proverb emphasises the
> importance of investing time and effort into adequate
> preparation before undertaking any significant endeavour.
> By doing so, potential issues, conflicts, or obstacles can

be addressed or mitigated in advance. This approach promotes a smoother and more successful process, allowing for a harmonious and conflict-free experience during the final stages of the fruition of the task or project. The proverb underscores the value of solid preparation and planning, emphasising that investing time and effort at the beginning stages of an undertaking can lead to a more prosperous and conflict-free outcome in the long run.

Xaman tepmek sündükning ishi emes.

Harvesting is not the job of a finch. (Kashgari 1072–74)
Literal Meaning: It suggests that individuals should focus on their strengths and skills rather than trying to undertake tasks that are beyond their capabilities or expertise. It encourages self-awareness and the acknowledgement of one's limitations, promoting the idea that each person has unique talents and contributions to offer. It serves as a reminder to stay within one's expertise and focus on tasks that align with one's skills and abilities. It emphasises the importance of recognising and respecting individual strengths and limitations to achieve successful outcomes.

Xatalashmighan danishmen nede?.

Where is the perfect sage?.
Idiomatic Meaning: If you don't make mistakes, you don't make anything.

Xelpet külmeydu, külse tëliqip qalidu.

Teacher does not laugh, and if he laughs, he cannot stop.
Idiomatic Meaning: It never rains but it pours.

Xelpet nëme ish qilidu? Tikip-söküp ish qilidu.

What does my teacher do? Works intermittently.
Idiomatic Meaning: Insanity is doing the same thing over and over, expecting different results.

Xotun kishi öy perishtisi.
> A wife is an angel of the home.
> **Literal Meaning: It** recognizes the important role that wives or spouses play in creating a loving and nurturing atmosphere within a family. It symbolises the qualities of care and support that are often associated with the role of a wife, but it's essential to acknowledge that the dynamics and contributions within a household can vary and should be based on the individual circumstances and values of the people involved.

Xotun kishi öyning güli.
> A wife is the flower of the house.
> **Idiomatic Meaning:** The grey mare is the better horse.

Xotunung bar öyüng gül, xotunung yoq öyüng chöl.
> With a wife, your home becomes a garden; without one, your home resembles a desert.
> **Literal Meaning:** The proverb "with a wife, your home becomes a garden; without one, your home resembles a desert" conveys the idea that having a loving and supportive wife contributes significantly to the happiness and harmony of a home while the absence of such a partner can lead to a feeling of emptiness or loneliness. It emphasises the value and importance of a harmonious marital relationship in creating a happy and fulfilling home environment. It suggests that a loving and supportive wife can significantly enrich one's life and contribute to a sense of contentment and well-being within the home. However, it is worth noting that this proverb reflects a traditional perspective and may not necessarily apply to every individual or family situation.

Xudayim bar ghemim yoq.
> As I have God, I have no worries.
> **Idiomatic Meaning:** All things are possible with God.

Xudayim qilar toqquz, men qilarmen ottuz.
God does nine, and I do thirty.
Idiomatic Meaning: Man proposes, God disposes.

Xudayimning etisi bar,.
God has tomorrow.
Idiomatic Meaning: Tomorrow is another day.

Xuyini bilmigen atning yënidin ötme.
Do not pass by a horse you do not know.
Idiomatic Meaning: Better the devil you know (than the devil you don't)

Ya Baydin chiq, ya Sayramdin (chiq)
Either get out of Bay[10], or get out of Sayram[11].
Idiomatic Meaning: A door must either be shut or open.

Yaghach kesseng uzun kes, tömür ketseng qisqa.
If you cut wood, cut it long; if you cut iron, cut it short.
(Kashgari 1072–74)
Literal Meaning: It conveys the importance of considering the characteristics and demands of different materials when undertaking tasks. It suggests adapting one's methods and techniques to achieve optimal results based on the specific properties and requirements of the material being worked with. It serves as a reminder to be mindful of the appropriate approach and strategy to accomplish tasks effectively and efficiently.

Yaghliq qapaq haman yaghliq qapaq.
Oily gourd ladles are always oily gourd ladles.
Idiomatic Meaning: once a priest, always a priest; once a whore, always a whore.

Yalghanchi bolghuche gacha bol.
Silence is better than telling a lie.

---

[10] A county in Uyghur region.
[11] A county in Uyghur region.

Literal Meaning: It highlights the importance of honesty and the potential benefits of refraining from dishonesty. It suggests that maintaining silence, when appropriate, can help uphold integrity and preserve trust in interpersonal relationships.

Yalghanchi yaljimas, oghri bëyimas.
A liar never flourishes; a thief never gets rich.
Idiomatic Meaning: Cheats never prosper; ill-gotten goods never thrive.

Yalghanchining quyruqi bir tutam,.
The tail of a liar is short.
Idiomatic Meaning: Cheats never prosper.

Yalghanchining risqi qisqa, ömri kötey.
The share of a liar is less; its life is short.
Idiomatic Meaning: cheats never prosper.

Yalghanchining wedisi (tügimes)
Liar's promise is endless.
Literal Meaning: It underscores the notion that a dishonest person can make empty promises without the intention to fulfil them, perpetuating a cycle of deception and unreliability. It serves as a reminder to be cautious and discerning in our interactions with others, ensuring that we trust those who demonstrate sincerity and integrity in their words and actions.

Yalghuz ghazning awazi chiqmas.
A single goose does not make a sound. (Kashgari 1072–74)
Literal Meaning: Just as a single goose may not make a significant sound, a person's actions or words may not have as much influence or attention. However, when people unite their voices or efforts towards a common goal, they can make a more robust and noticeable impact. This proverb highlights the importance of collaboration, teamwork, and collective action. It encourages individuals

to join forces, speak up, and work collectively to achieve
desired outcomes or bring about positive change. It
emphasises the strength and effectiveness of unity and
cooperation over individual efforts.

Yaman'gha ölüm yoq, yaxshigha körüm (yoq)
There is no death for evil; the good die young.
Idiomatic Meaning: The good die young.

Yamanliqqa yamanliq.
Evil for evil.
Idiomatic Meaning: Evil begets evil.

Yandiki mollam, bar mollam, yiraqtiki mollam damollam.
The mullah always appears better in other people's
villages.
Idiomatic Meaning: The grass is always greener on the
other side of the fence; a prophet is not recognised in his
own land.

Yaqisidin yalaymen dep, ilikidikidin ayriliptu.
He lost the meal in his hand to lick the crumbs on his
collar. (Kashgari 1072–74)
Literal Meaning: It serves as a cautionary reminder to
prioritise wisely and avoid getting distracted by trivial
matters that may divert attention from more important
goals, responsibilities, or opportunities. It suggests the
need to focus on what truly matters and not be consumed
by insignificant distractions.

Yashliqingda bilim al, qërighanda ishqa sal.
Learn in your youth, reap in your old age.
Literal Meaning: It underscores the significance of early
learning and its long-lasting impact on personal and
professional growth. It encourages individuals to embrace
a lifelong learning mindset and reap the benefits of their
accumulated knowledge and skills.

Yat yëgiche, tughqan ölgiche.
A stranger's loyalty ends with the meal; a relative's lasts a
lifetime.
Idiomatic Meaning: Blood is thicker than water.

Yatning yaghliq loqmisidin özining qanliq mushti yaxshi.
My bloody fist is better than a stranger's delicious bite.
(Kashgari 1072–74)
Literal Meaning: It suggests that achieving something
through personal effort, despite difficulties or challenges,
carries a sense of accomplishment and pride. It implies
that the satisfaction and sense of ownership from working
hard and earning something outweigh the temporary
pleasure or convenience of receiving something from
others without any personal investment.

Yatqan ëshekning poqi torluq.
Lazy donkey's dung is heavy.
Idiomatic Meaning: Much cry and little wool.

Yatqan itqa tash atma.
Do not throw stones at a lying dog.
Idiomatic Meaning: Let sleeping dogs lie.

Yatqan yilanni oyghatma.
Do not wake the sleeping snake.
Idiomatic Meaning: Let sleeping dogs lie.

Yaxshi adem ishidin melum.
A good man is known for the job he does.
Literal Meaning: It emphasises the idea that a person's
character and worth can be assessed by observing the
quality of their work or the way they carry out their
responsibilities.

Yaxshi ademning söngiki chirisimu, nami qalidu.
A good man's bones rot, but his name endures. (Kashgari
1072–74)
Literal Meaning: It highlights the enduring legacy and

reputation of a person who lived a virtuous and
honourable life, even after their physical existence ends.

Yaxshi atqa bir qamcha, yaman atqa ming qamcha.
A good horse needs a whip, but a lousy horse needs a
thousand.
Idiomatic Meaning: A word to the wise is enough.

Yaxshi atqa qamcha ketmes.
A good horse needs no whip.
Idiomatic Meaning: Good wine needs no bush.

***Yaxshi bilen dost bolsang, ëchilar chëchekliring. Yaman
bilen dost bolsang yërilar* yürekliring.**
If you befriend goodness, your flowers will bloom. If you
befriend evil, your heart will be broken.
Idiomatic Meaning: A man is known by the company he
keeps.

Yaxshi gep tashni yarar, yaman gep bashni.
A good word splits a stone, and a bad word breaks one's
head.
Idiomatic Meaning: Honey catches more flies than
vinegar.

Yaxshi mëhman ash üstige këlidu.
A good visitor will come when the good food is served.
Literal Meaning: It acknowledges the timing of the
guest's arrival in a positive and welcoming manner,
expressing appreciation for their presence. It sets a warm
and inviting tone, allowing the guests to feel included and
comfortable as they partake in the meal.

Yaxshi söz qedehke ige qilur.
A good speech deserves the salute. (Kashgari 1072–74)
Literal Meaning: A good speech often receives a salute
or is deserving of recognition and appreciation. When
someone delivers an eloquent, persuasive, or inspiring

speech, the audience often responds with applause, admiration, or other forms of acknowledgement.

Yaxshi xewer ishiktin chiqquche, yaman xewer dawan eshiptu.
Before the good news reaches the door, the bad news has already crossed the hill.
Idiomatic Meaning: Bad news travels fast; a lie is halfway around the world before the truth has got its boots on.

Yaxshi xotun – öy berikiti.
The good wife is the blessing of the house.
Literal Meaning: It emphasises the importance of a virtuous and supportive wife in creating a nurturing and happy home environment. It highlights the role of a wife as a source of blessings, love, and harmony within the family unit.

Yaxshi xotun – öyge qozuq.
A good wife is the foundation of the family.
Literal Meaning: It acknowledges a wife's essential role in establishing a solid and harmonious family unit. It highlights her contributions to nurturing relationships, managing household affairs, and providing emotional support. However, it is essential to recognise that a successful family relies on all its members' collective efforts, mutual respect, and shared responsibilities.

Yaxshi xotun erni er qilar yaman, yaman xotun yaxshi erni yer qilar.
A good wife makes a man a gentleman; a poor wife spoils even the best.
Literal Meaning: It reflects the belief in the influence of a wife's character and behaviour on her husband. It underscores the importance of positive influences and values within a marital relationship. However, it should be understood within the context of evolving societal

norms and the recognition of mutual responsibilities and individual agency in relationships.

Yaxshi xotun öyning chirighi, yaxshi bala öyning zinniti.
A good wife is the light of the house, and a good child is the ornament of the house.
Idiomatic Meaning: The grey mare is the better horse.

Yaxshi xulq yërim dölet.
A good character is half a fortune.
Idiomatic Meaning: Better a good cow than a cow of a good kind.

Yaxshigha egeshseng gösh yeysen, yaman'gha egeshseng mush (yeysen)
If you follow the good, you will feast on meat; if you follow the bad, you will receive a fist.
Idiomatic Meaning: When the blind lead the blind, both shall fall into a ditch.

Yaxshiliq yerde qalmas.
Goodness shall not perish.
Idiomatic Meaning: Kindness, like a boomerang, always returns.

Yaxshiliqqa yaxshiliq.
Goodness begets goodness.
Idiomatic Meaning: One good turn deserves another.

Yaz bolsa, qish bolmisa, ash bolsa ish (bolmisa)
I wish there were only summer, no winter, only food, with no need for work.
Idiomatic Meaning: The cat would eat fish but would not wet her feet.

Yekcheshmining shehirige barsang bir közüngni qisiwal.
If you go to the city of cyclopes, close your eyes.
Idiomatic Meaning: When in Rome, do as the Romans do.

Yekke qoldin chawak chiqmas.
A single hand cannot clap.
Idiomatic Meaning: It takes two to make a quarrel; It takes two to tango.

Yëmiseng ach qalisen, ögenmiseng këyin qalisen.
If you do not eat, you starve; if you do not learn, you fall behind.
Literal Meaning: It emphasises the importance of physical nourishment and intellectual growth. Neglecting either aspect can hinder our progress and limit our potential. It encourages individuals to prioritise their physical and intellectual needs to thrive and succeed.

Yëngi kölning süyi tatliq.
The water of the new lake is sweet.
Idiomatic Meaning: New brooms sweep clean.

Yëngi küpning süyi soghuq.
The water of the new clay pots is cold.
Idiomatic Meaning: New brooms sweep clean.

Yette ölchep bir kes.
Measure seven times and cut once.
Idiomatic Meaning: Look before you leap, measure seven times, cut once; Measure twice, cut once; think twice, cut once.

Yighlighandin qorqma, külgendin qorq.
Do not fear the one who weeps; fear the one who laughs.
Idiomatic Meaning: Beware of Greeks bearing gifts.

Yighlimighan bowaqqa ëmizge salma.
Do not give a dummy to a baby who has not cried.
Idiomatic Meaning: Don't mend what ain't broken; if it ain't broke, don't fix it.

Yighlimisa emchek salmaydu.
One will not breastfeed the baby unless it cries.

Idiomatic Meaning: Don't mend what ain't broken; If it ain't broke, don't fix it.

Yighsang qummu tagh bolidu.
Through the collection, even grains of sand can amass into a mountain.
Literal Meaning: This proverb implies that by consistently and persistently working towards a goal, even the most minor efforts can accumulate and lead to significant achievements. It emphasises the power of continuous dedication and the potential for substantial results, likening the gradual accumulation of sand grains to the formation of a grand mountain.

Yipeklik yamaq yipek rextke, yung yamaq yung rextke layiq këlidu.
A silk patch befits silk fabric, while a wool patch suits woollen material. (Kashgari 1072–74)
Literal Meaning: This proverb suggests that it is best to match or tailor the solution or remedy to the specific nature of the problem or situation. Just as a silk patch is most suitable for repairing silk fabric and a wool patch is best for fixing woollen material, it emphasises the importance of using the right tools, approaches, or strategies most appropriate and effective for a particular context. It highlights the value of precision and customisation in addressing different needs.

Yiqilghan chëlishqa toymaptu.
Defeated wrestlers will always ask for more.
Literal Meaning: The proverb encourages individuals to embrace challenges, learn from failures, and strive for improvement. It highlights that setbacks are not the end but stepping stones towards future accomplishments.

Yiraq yer xewirini karwan keltürer.
A caravan brings news from a distant land. (Kashgari 1072–74)

Literal Meaning: The proverb suggests that travellers or groups who journey from one place to another, such as a caravan, often bring information, stories, or news from distant or faraway lands. It implies that knowledge and information about other places and cultures are exchanged through the movement and interaction of people across different regions. It encourages a spirit of curiosity, openness, and the exploration of new horizons, both literal and metaphorical, to expand one's understanding of the world and benefit from the insights and experiences brought by others.

Yiraqtin qarisam eldin artuq, yëqindin qarisam Hashim tartuq.
From afar, beauty beckons; up close, Quasimodo awaits.
Idiomatic Meaning: Distance lends enchantment to the view.

Yoldin chiqma, xandin qorma.
Stand your ground; fear not the king.
Idiomatic Meaning: Do right and fear no man.

Yoldin chiqma, xandin[12] qorqma.
Abide by the law, and no khan shall bring fear.
Idiomatic Meaning: Do right and fear no man.

Yolni karwandin sora.
Seek guidance from the caravan.
Idiomatic Meaning: To know the road ahead ask those coming back.

Yotqandin artuq put sunulsa üshshüydu.
Do not extend your legs beyond the length of your blanket, or you will get a cold. (Kashgari 1072–74)
Literal Meaning: The proverb encourages individuals to

---

[12] A title historically used in Central Asia and the Middle East to denote a leader or chieftain. In modern times, it is also a common surname in South Asia and Central Asia, reflecting its historical and cultural significance.

be mindful of their actions, consider the limitations or boundaries that are in place, and exercise moderation and restraint. It promotes balancing ambition and practicality, avoiding unnecessary risks or actions that may have adverse effects. It serves as a reminder to respect boundaries, exercise caution, and avoid actions that may lead to undesirable outcomes. It emphasises the importance of maintaining a sense of proportion and understanding the consequences of exceeding one's limits.

Yotqan'gha bëqip put sun.
Stretch your legs within the bounds of your coverlet.
Idiomatic Meaning: Stretch your arms no further than your sleeve will reach; do not bite off more than you can chew.

Yükini kötergen töge chömüchnimu köturidu.
A camel that carries a burden also can carry a pitcher. (Kashgari 1072–74)
Literal Meaning: metaphorically, the proverb conveys that individuals who have successfully tackled significant challenges or responsibilities can easily manage smaller ones. The proverb underscores the concept of capability and resilience, emphasising that those who have shouldered substantial burdens are well-equipped to handle smaller tasks or additional demands without being overwhelmed.

Yurt qalar, törü qalmas.
The land will remain, but customs may change. (Kashgari 1072–74)
Literal Meaning: The proverb suggests that while the land and its geographical boundaries remain constant, the customs and traditions associated with it may evolve, adapt, or even disappear over time. It reflects the notion of cultural change, emphasising that societal practices are subject to transformation as people, generations, and external influences contribute to the evolution of customs.

The proverb highlights the enduring nature of the homeland itself while acknowledging the potential evolution and transformation of customs and traditions. It emphasises embracing change and growth while maintaining a sense of attachment and connection to the land.

Yüzige qarima, erdimini tile.
Do not judge by appearances; seek the virtues within. (Kashgari 1072–74)
Literal Meaning: The proverb reminds us to look beyond the surface and not judge individuals solely based on their outward appearance. It encourages a deeper understanding and appreciation of people based on their virtues and inner qualities, highlighting the importance of character and substance over physical attributes.

Zaman öter, kishi tuymas, adem balisi menggü qalmas.
Time slips away unnoticed, and no one is eternal. (Kashgari 1072–74)
Literal Meaning: It conveys a sense of urgency and the need to make the most of our time. It encourages us to be mindful of the passing of time and make the most of our opportunities and experiences. It serves as a reminder to appreciate the present moment and prioritise what is truly important in our lives, as time is a precious and finite resource.

Zaman qëritqan'gha boyaq eyib emes.
The paint is not to blame for the effects of ageing caused by the passage of time. (Kashgari 1072–74)
Literal Meaning: It encourages acceptance and understanding of the ageing process and recognises that true beauty and value come from within rather than relying solely on external appearances. It serves as a reminder to embrace the passage of time and appreciate the wisdom and experiences that come with it rather than trying to fight or deny the natural aging process.

Zaman sanga baqmisa, sen zaman'gha baq.
When time refuses to conform to your desires, adjust to its rhythm.
Idiomatic Meaning: If the mountain does not come to Mahomet, Mahomet must go to the mountain.

Zorluq-zombuluq ishiktin kirse, insap we qaide-yosun tünglüktin chiqar.
As violence enters, discipline and manners depart through the window. (Kashgari 1072–74)
Literal Meaning: It highlights violence's disruptive and destructive nature on order, discipline, and proper behaviour. The proverb encourages peaceful resolutions, cultivates self-discipline, and preserves good manners and respect, even in the face of provocation or aggression. It serves as a reminder of the negative consequences of violence on social interactions and the need to uphold the values of civility and restraint.

English- Uyghur

Abide by the law, and no khan shall bring fear.
Yoldin chiqma, xandin qorqma.
Idiomatic meaning: do right and fear no man.

Accept destiny.
Teqdirge ten ber.
Idiomatic meaning: What can't be cured must be endured.

Be accountable for your actions and avoid calling your neighbour a thief.
Özüngni ching tut, xoshangni oghri tutma.
Idiomatic meaning: Good fences make good neighbours.

To acquire knowledge, acknowledge your ignorance.
Bilim alay dёseng, özüngning bilimsiz ikenlikini iqrar qil.

Acquiring knowledge is worth more than amassing gold.
Bilim ёlish altun yighishtinmu artuq.

Actions open the door to flourishing; sincerity lights the path to enlightenment.
heriket qilsang beriket taparsen, ixlas qilsang meripet taparsen,.
Idiomatic meaning: seek and you shall find.

An active doer surpasses ten mere speakers.
on gepchidin bir ishchan ela.
Idiomatic meaning: actions speak louder than words; fine words, butter, no parsnips.

Adventure can splIt the stone.
Tewekkül tash yaridu.
Idiomatic meaning: Adventures are for the adventurous.

All that glitters is not gold.
Paqirghanning hemhisi altun emes.
Idiomatic meaning: all that glitters is not gold.

Allowing water to flow under wheat hay.
samanning tëgidin su quyuptu.

Amidst many, wisdom thrives.
Köpning eqli köp.
Idiomatic meaning: many hands make light work; so
many heads so many wits; two heads are better than one.

Anger drives the wits away.
Achchiq eqilni këser.

Animal colours show; man's true colours hide.
Ademning alisi ichide, buyrusang alisi tëshida.

An apology is always a companion to the ignorant.
Bilimsizge pushayman hemrah.

An archer's renown rests on their aim, not their bow.
Mergen oqyasi bilen emes, mergenliki bilen dangliq.

**An armpIt cannot hold two watermelons, and a foot
cannot stand on two boats simultaneously**.
*Ikki tawuzni bir qoltuqqa qisqili bolmas, ikki këmige teng
dessigili bolmas.*
Idiomatic meaning: if you run after two hares you will
catch neither.

Never assume a dog will not bite or a horse will not kick.
It chishlimes, at tepmes dëme.

To attain wisdom, you must invest in books.
Eqil tapay dëseng kitab al.

Autumn reveals itself through the traces of summer.
Küzning qandaq këlishi yazdin melum bolidu.

Avoid praising your riches in the company of a thief.
Oghrining aldida pul - mëlingni maxtima.

Bald's wisdom appears in the afternoon.
Tazning eqli chüshtin këyin.
Idiomatic meaning: it is easy to be wise after the event.

Beautiful is not beautiful; love is beautiful.
Chirayliq chirayliq emes, köygen chirayliq.
Idiomatic meaning: Beauty is in the eye of the beholder.

A beautiful man possesses a beautiful manner.
Özi chirayliqning qiliqi chirayliq.
Idiomatic meaning: handsome is as handsome does;
manners maketh the man.

Beauty is not in a face but in words (actions)
Chirayliq yüzde emes, sözde.
Idiomatic meaning: beauty is only skin-deep.

Beauty is not nourished by sipping tea.
Chirayigha nan chilap ichkili bolmaydu.
Idiomatic meaning: Appearances can be deceptive.

Because of wheat, the cowherb waters itself.
Bughdayning bahaniside, qarimuq su ichiptu.
Idiomatic meaning: R rising tide lifts all boats.

A bee has a sting; a flower has a thorn.
Heselning herisi bar, gülning tikini.
Idiomatic meaning: no rose without a thorn; every rose
has its thorn.

**Before an elder's anger ignites, young souls blaze with
fury.**
Chongning achchiqi kelgüche, kichikning jëni chiqiptu.
Idiomatic meaning: a little pot is soon hot.

**Before the good news reaches the door, the bad news has
already crossed the hill.**
*Yaxshi xewer ishiktin chiqquche, yaman xewer dawan
eshiptu.*
Idiomatic meaning: bad news travels fast; a lie is

halfway round the world before the truth has got its boots on.

Before the large loaf was baked, the small loaf was charred.
Chong nan pishqiche, kichik toqach köyüp boptu.
Idiomatic meaning: a little pot is soon hot.

A beggar does not choose.
Abdal tallimas.
Idiomatic meaning: Beggars can't be choosers.

Beneath a tattered coat resides a gentleman.
Eski chapanning ichide er bar.

It is better to argue with a dog for a bone than to involve oneself with an evil man.
Eski bilen gep talashqiche, it bilen söngek talashqan yaxshi.

Better to catch fire than be a guarantor.
Këpil bolghuche, ot tut.

It is better to pick your nose than to pick fault in others.
Kishining eyibini kolighuche, özüngning burnini kola.

Big fish eat the little fish.
Chong bëliq kichik bëliqni yeptu.
Idiomatic meaning: Big fish eat little fish.

A bird will land on a branchy willow, and suitors will come to a beautiful girl.
Bük-baraqsan sögetke qush qonar, chirayliq qizgha söz këler.

A bird find its trap in the lure of bait.
Qush tuzaqqa yem üchün iliner.

The blessing of a house stems from the wife's care, just as the blessing of a pot arises from the wood's

contribution.
Öyning berikiti xotundin, qazanning berikiti otundin.
Idiomatic meaning: the grey mare is the better horse.

Blood cannot cleanse the blood.
qanni qan bilen yughili bolmas.

Both a dog and a gossip cling tightly to their bones.
Itning aghzidin söngek ashmas, gheywetxorning aghzidin gep (ashmas)
Idiomatic meaning: A dog that will fetch a bone will carry a bone.

The bowed head escapes the sword's cut.
Ëgilgen bashni qilich kesmeptu.
Idiomatic meaning: better is to bow then breake.

A bread in time saves nine.
Waqtida bergen nan ölükke kirgen jan.
Idiomatic meaning: A stitch in time saves nine.

If breath remains, hope perseveres.
Ölmigen janda ümid bar.
Idiomatic meaning: while there's life, there's hope; hope springs eternal.

Bribery opens the gates of hell.
Dozaqning ishikini para achidu.

The budget at home does not align with the market.
Öydiki hësab bazargha yarimaptu.

Build a levee before the river's surge.
su kelgüche toghan sal.
Idiomatic meaning: Prevention is better than cure.

The calf of a black pied cattle bears a short tail.
Ala inekning balisi, chala quyruq.
Idiomatic meaning: like mother, like daughter; like father, like son.

Being a calf's head is better than a cow's hoof.
*Öküzning ayighi bolghiche, mozayning bëshi bolghan
yaxshi.*

A camel is lost for want of a button.
Tügmini dep tögidin quruq qaptu.
Idiomatic meaning: a kingdom is lost for want of a shoe.

A camel rider cannot hide among sheep.
Töge minip qoy arisigha yoshurunalmas.

A camel that carries a burden also can carry a pitcher.
Yükini kötergen töge chömüchnimu köturidu.

A caravan brings news from a distant land.
Yiraq yer xewirini karwan keltürer.

Cash is better than credit.
Nësidin neq yaxshi.
Idiomatic meaning: a live dog is better than a dead lion.

Cheap meat produces thin broth.
Erzan göshning shorpisi tëtimas.

Chicks chirp what they know.
Chüje xoraz bilginini chillaydu.
Idiomatic meaning: shoemaker, not above the sandal.

A child shall be born resembling their father.
Ata balisi atisidek tughular.
Idiomatic meaning: like father like son; the apple never
falls far from the tree.

The chimney knows the bitterness of the smoke.
Tütünning derdini mora bilidu.

Cleanliness comes from faith.
Pakizlik imandin kelidu.
Idiomatic meaning: cleanliness is next to Godliness.

Clergymen's son is belligerent.
Mollamning oghli urushqaq.
Idiomatic meaning: clergymen's sons always turn out badly; the apple doesn't fall far from the tree.

Clothes embellish a man, while a saddle adorns a horse.
Kiyim ademning zinniti, iger atning (zinniti)
Idiomatic meaning: clothes maketh the man.

Clothes make the man, while leaves define the tree.
Adem zinniti kiyim, derex qimmiti yopurmaq.
Idiomatic meaning: clothes maketh the man.

Conceal the ailment, and the truth of mortality shall be unveiled.
Këselni yoshursang, ölümi ashkare.
Idiomatic meaning: love and a cough cannot be hid.

He confidently dines on the road when the merchant's earnings are clean.
Sodigerning ozuqi ërigh bolsa, yol üstide yer.

The confines of my own home hold the essence of contentment, where my feet find solace, and my hands find joy.
Öz öyümning boshluqi, put - qolumning xoshluqi.
Idiomatic meaning: there is no place like home.

Cool the head and warm the feet for a healthy body and a soul's retreat.
Bëshingni salqin, putungni issiq tut, tenning saqliqi, janning rahiti.
Idiomatic meaning: the head and feet keep warm, the rest will take no harm.

The counsel may be bitter, but its fruIt bears sweetness.
Nesihet achchiq, mëwisi tatliq.
Idiomatic meaning: bitter pills may have blessed effects.

Counselled work will not go wrong.
Këngeshlik ish buzulmas.

Count not others' wealth as your own.
özge kishining mali, mal sanalmas.

Count the chicken in the fall, (count) the ravioli when they are cooked.
Chüjini küzde sanang, chöchürini pishqanda (sanang)
Idiomatic meaning: don't count your chickens before they hatch.

A coward dies a thousand times without dying.
Qorqunchaq ölmey turup ming qëtim öler.
Idiomatic meaning: cowards die many times before their death. The valiant never taste of death but once.

The craft of silent man is hidden within.
Jimghurning hüniri ichide.
Idiomatic meaning: a clever hawk hides its claws; a still tongue makes a wise head.

Craftiness may snare a lion, yet force cannot conquer a scarecrow.
Hile bilen arslan tutular, küch bilen qaranchuqmu tutulmas.

A crooked twig begets a crooked tree.
Egri köchettin egri derex chiqar.
Idiomatic meaning: as the twig is bent, so is the tree inclined.

A crow does not peck another crow's eye.
Qagha qaghining közini choqimaydu.
Idiomatic meaning: hawks will not pick out hawks' eyes.

The crow adores her white child, and the hedgehog treasures her soft baby.
Qagha balam ap'aq balam, kirpe balam yumshaq (balam)

Death pursues the frightened.
  Qorqqanni ejel qoghlar.
  Idiomatic meaning: courage lost, all lost.

Deep streams run still.
  Chongqur östeng asta aqidu.
  Idiomatic meaning: deep waters run still.

Defeated wrestler will always ask for more.
  Yiqilghan chëlishqa toymaptu.

Desiring demise, the mouse snared the cat's tail.
  Ölgüsi kelgen chashqan, müshükning quyruqigha ësiliptu.

Despite the concealed axe in the heart, laughter lingers upon the lips.
  Aghzida külke - chaqchaq, qoynida palta – pichaq.

Do It if you can, or gracefully let It go if you cannot.
  Qilalsang qil, bolmisa boldi qil.
  Idiomatic meaning: shit or get off the pot.

Do not ask questions of a tired person or a hungry man.
  Bir harghandin, bir achqandin gep sorima.
  Idiomatic meaning: the belly has no ears.

Do not break the pot that feeds you.
  Ash bergen qazanni chaqma.
  Idiomatic meaning: don't bite the hand that feeds you.

Do not consume whatever comes your way, nor speak whatever your mind may say.
  Aldimgha keldi dep yëme, aghzimgha keldi dep dëme.

Do not embrace fruitless trees, nor rest in dubious spaces.
  Mëwisiz derexni qaqma, gumanliq yerde yatma.

Do not engage in battle with a maiden nor race against a spirited mare.
  Qiz bilen chëlishma, baytal bilen chëpishma.

Idiomatic meaning: The grey mare is the better horse; the female of the species is more deadly than the male.

Do not lead a wolf to the sheepfold.
Börini qotangha bashlima.
Idiomatic meaning: do not call a wolf to help you against the dogs.

Do not pretend to know what you do not know.
Bilmigenni bilimen dep kayima.
Idiomatic meaning: let the cobbler stick to his last.

Do not spIt at the well from which you have quenched your thirst.
Su ichken quduqqa tükürme.

Do not wake the sleeping snake.
Yatqan yilanni oyghatma.
Idiomatic meaning: let sleeping dogs lie.

Dog barks, and the caravan goes on.
It hürer, karwan yürer.
Idiomatic meaning: dogs bark, but the caravan goes on.

A dog that barks does not bite, but a dog that bites may lurk in shadows.
Qawighan it chishlimeydu, chishleydighan it maraydu.
Idiomatic meaning: a barking dog never bites; barking dogs seldom bite.

Dog that is tied is not fIt for hunting.
Baghlaqtiki it - owgha yarimaptu.
Idiomatic meaning: a cat in gloves catches no mice.

Dog's habits are set in stone.
It - itliqini qilmisa köngli tinmas.
Idiomatic meaning: the dog returns to its vomit.

Don't leave today's work for tomorrow.
Bügünki ishni etige qoyma.

Idiomatic meaning: never put off till tomorrow what you can do today.

Don't spend your time idly, and spend your money wisely.
Bikar yürme laghaylap, pulni xejle awaylap.
Idiomatic meaning: what you spend, you have.

Don't dig into the faults of the dead.
Ölgenning eyibini kolima.
Idiomatic meaning: never speak ill of the dead.

Don't do what you don't know; share what you know.
Bilmigenni qilma, bilginingni ayima.
Idiomatic meaning: let the cobbler stick to his last.

Don't extend your legs beyond the length of your blanket, or you'll catch a cold.
Yotqandin artuq put sunulsa üshshüydu.

Don't fear the one who weeps; fear the one who laughs.
Yighlighandin qorqma, külgendin qorq.
Idiomatic meaning: beware of greeks bearing gifts.

Don't hIt the egg on the stone.
Tuxumni tashqa urma.
Idiomatic meaning: do not spoil the ship for a ha'porth of tar.

Don't judge by appearances, seek the virtues within.
Yüzige qarima, erdimini tile.

Do not give a dummy to a baby who has not cried.
Yighlimighan bowaqqa ëmizge salma.
Idiomatic meaning: Don't mend what ain't broken; If it ain't broke, don't fix it.

Don't pass by a horse you don't know.
Xuyini bilmigen atning yënidin ötme.
Idiomatic meaning: better the devil you know (than the devil you don't)

Don't play with fire.
> *Ot bilen oynashma,.*
> **Idiomatic meaning:** do not play with fire.

Don't remove your boots until the water's in sight.
> *Suni körmey ötük salma.*
> **Idiomatic meaning:** don't halloo till you are out of the wood; don't sell the skin till you have caught the bear.

Don't sacrifice the chicken in your coop for the elusive pheasant in the field.
> *Qirdiki qirghawulni owlaymen dep, öydiki toxuni qoldin chiqirip qoyma.*

Don't scorch the quilt to banish the lice.
> *pitning achchiqida chapanni ochaqqa salma!.*
> **Idiomatic meaning:** don't throw the baby out with the bathwater.

Don't throw stones at a lying dog.
> *Yatqan itqa tash atma.*
> **Idiomatic meaning:** let sleeping dogs lie.

Don't you have a kind word, even if you don't have wheat bread?.
> *Bughday nëning bolmisa, bughday sözüng yoqmidi?.*
> **Idiomatic meaning:** say something nice or say nothing at all.

As the door's size determines its lock, your behaviour reflects mine in stock.
> *sanga bëqip men, ishikke bëqip dem.*
> **Idiomatic meaning:** the door swings both ways; circumstances alter cases.

Dreams go by contraries.
> *Chüsh tetürige mangidu.*
> **Idiomatic meaning:** dreams go by contraries.

Drops make a lake.
> *Tama - tama köl bolar.*
> **Idiomatic meaning:** little strokes fell great oaks; many a little makes a mickle.

Drops of water pierce a stone.
> *Tamche su tashni tësher.*
> **Idiomatic meaning:** constant dropping wears away a stone.

Each flower has its own smell.
> *Her gülning özige chüshlüq puriqi bar,.*
> **Idiomatic meaning:** each to his own taste.

Earn wisdom before you earn money.
> *Pup tapquche eqil tap.*
> **Idiomatic meaning:** a fool and his money are soon parted.

Eat the grapes, ask not the brunch.
> *Üzümni ye, sapiqini sorima.*
> **Idiomatic meaning:** never look a gift horse in the mouth.

An educated son surpasses his father.
> *Oqughan oghul atisidin ela.*
> **Idiomatic meaning:** learning is better than house and land.

An eggless chicken surpasses a powerless sufi.
> *Emili yoq sopidin tuxumi yoq toxu yaxshi.*
> **Idiomatic meaning:** better are small fish than an empty dish.

Either get out of Bay[13], or get out of Sayram[14].
Ya Baydin chiq, ya Sayramdin (chiq)
Idiomatic meaning: a door must either be shut or open.

Elderly people's words were said not in vain.
Qërilar sözi bikar ketmes.

An elevated tail of a cow foretells the presence of dung.
Quyruqini kötürgen kala chichmay qalmaptu.
Idiomatic meaning: if anything can go wrong, it will.

Embrace it, even if It is meagre.
Az bolsimu köpke tawap qil.
Idiomatic meaning: every little helps.

Embrace the calamity, and with patience, endure the disaster.
Qazagha riza, balagha sewri.
Idiomatic meaning: bear and forbear.

Empty buckets sound aloud, the ignorant roars.
Quruq chëlek taraqlaydu, nadan walaqlaydu.
Idiomatic meaning: empty vessels make the most sound.

An empty sack doesn't stand upright.
Bosh taghar öre turmas.

Empty sack doesn't stand upright.
Quruq/bosh taghar öre turmaydu.
Idiomatic meaning: empty sacks will never stand upright.

The enemy of your enemy is your friend.
Düshminingning düshmini sëning dostung.
Idiomatic meaning: the enemy of my enemy is my friend,.

---

[13] A county in Uyghur region.
[14] A county in Uyghur region.

Entrapped by the allure of sweet words, man becomes a captive.
Sözge mezze qilsa, tutqun bolur.

Escaping the mud, he plunged into the swamp.
Patqaqtin qutulup, sazliqqa kirip qaptu.
Idiomatic meaning: out of the frying pan into the fire.

Even a mountain bows to the might of many.
Köpning küchige, taghmu teng këlelmes.
Idiomatic meaning: when spider webs unite, they can tie up a lion.

Even amidst a flooded world, why should the duck be concerned?.
Dunyani su bassa, ördekke nëme ghem.

Even if your horse is like your father, tie It up before you rest.
At atangche bolsimu at, yerge qozuq qëqip baghlap yat.
Idiomatic meaning: trust in God but tie your camel.

Every heart knows its own sorrow.
herkim öz ölüki üchün yighlar.

Everyone has value.
Her kimning qimmiti bar.
Idiomatic meaning: every man has his price.

Everyone's destiny is in their own hands.
Her kimning qedri öz qolida.
Idiomatic meaning: every man is the architect of his own fortune.

Everyone's lover is beautiful.
Her kimning söygini özige chirayliq.
Idiomatic meaning: every man to his taste.

There is no death for evil, the good person dies young.
> *Yaman'gha ölüm yoq, yaxshigha körüm (yoq)*
> **Idiomatic meaning:** the good die young.

Evil for evil.
> *Yamanliqqa yamanliq.*
> **Idiomatic meaning:** evil begets evil.

Excessive excitement paves the way to regret.
> *Köp söyünüp ketse, qattiq öküner.*

Excessive talk burdens the donkey's load.
> *Artuq gep, ëshekke yük.*
> **Idiomatic meaning:** brag is a good dog, but holdfast is a better.

The face of a thief reveals a duality of darkness.
> *Oghrining ikki yüzi qara.*
> **Idiomatic meaning:** there is honour among thieves.

A familiar devil is better than a stranger.
> *Tonush emes kishidin, tonush sheytan yaxshi.*

A familiar tree bears many twigs.
> *Tonush yaghachning putiqi köp.*

Don't have five fingers in your mouth.
> *Besh qolni bir yoli aghzigha tiqqili bolmas.*
> **Idiomatic meaning:** don't have too many irons in the fire.

Fire cannot be contained by cotton.
> *Paxta ichide ot saqlighili bolmas.*

The fish resides in the water yet keeps its eyes beyond.
> *Bëliqning özi suda, közi tashqirida.*

Five fingers are uneven.
> *Besh barmaq tekshi emes.*

A flame cannot extinguish a fire.
Otni yalqun bilen öchürgili bolmas.

Flesh cannot be separated from the nails.
Et tirnaqtin ayrilmas.

Flowing water doesn't stink.
Aqar su purimaydu.

Fly in haste falls into the milk.
Aldiraqsan chiwin sütke chüsher.
Idiomatic meaning: hasty climbers have sudden falls.

Follow a clergyman's words, not his actions.
Mollining dëginini qil, qilghinini qilma.
Idiomatic meaning: do as i say, not as i do.

A fool comes in all sizes.
Exmeq chong-kichiki yoq.

A foolish apostle will destroy both sides.
Exmeq elchi ikki terepni buzar.

A foolish fox meets its end, caught by its beak.
Nadan tülke tumshuqidin ilinar.
Idiomatic meaning: fools rush in where angels fear to
tread.

Fools are not defined by their age.
Exmeqning chong - kichiki bolmas.
Idiomatic meaning: a fool at forty is a fool indeed.

Fool's hands are long, but his mind is short.
Exmeqning qoli uzun, eqli qisqa.
Idiomatic meaning: a fool and his money are soon
parted.

For a lazy, cloud shadows are a burden.
Ërinchekke bulut kölenggisi yuk bolur.

For the lazy, even a sill becomes a hill.
Ërinchekke bosughimu dawan körüner.

The foundation of labour is comfort.
Mëhnetning tëgi rahet.
Idiomatic meaning: crosses are ladders that lead to heaven.

Fox does not admire the swiftness of a hound.
Tayghanning yügürükini tülke söymes.

Fresh air is a cure for the body.
Sap hawa, ten'ge dawa.

A friend praises you behind your back; an enemy only praises you in front of you.
Dost keyningde maxtar, düshmen aldingda (maxtar)

A friend's true friendship shines when you are in need.
Dostning dostluqi bashqa kün chüshkende biliner.
Idiomatic meaning: a friend in need is a friend indeed.

Don't disregard a friend's words; if you do, don't be surprised by the consequences.
Dost sözini tashlima, tashlap beshingni qashlima.

An enemy steals your secrets; a friend corrects your errors.
Düshmen siringni oghrilaydu, dost xatayingni toghrilaydu.

Excessive talk leads to trouble, while silence offers safety.
Tola sözligen tutular, az sözligen qutular.
Idiomatic meaning: least said, soonest mended.

A frightened man sees a sheep's head as double.
Qorqqan kishige qoy bëshi qosh körüner.

From afar, beauty beckons; up close, Quasimodo awaits.
Yiraqtin qarisam eldin artuq, yëqindin qarisam hashim

tartuq.
Idiomatic meaning: distance lends enchantment to the view.

From the moment of birth, kittens arrive with purrs.
Müshük balisi miyanglap tughular.
Idiomatic meaning: the apple never falls far from the tree.

Fruitful trees bow, gaining support; fruitless trees stand tall, facing the axe.
Mëwilik derex ëgilip turidu, kishiler anga tërek qoyidu.
Mëwisiz derex ghadiyip turidu, kishiler uni putap turidu.
Idiomatic meaning: the nail that sticks up will be hammered down.

The full moon needs no hand to be revealed.
Ay tolun bolsa, qol bilen imlenmes.
Idiomatic meaning: the point is plain as a pike staff.

The full moon needs no manual indication.
Tolun ay qol bilen körsitilmes.

Gaggle can't be leaderless.
Ghaz topi bashlamchisiz bolmas.

There is no crack in the sun nor break in the gentlemen's promise.
Künde yëriq yoq, begde yëniwëlish yoq.

Give a sycophant wings, and they'll soar beyond their realm; adorn a servant with jewels, and they'll explore every corner of their realm.
Ghalcha at minse chiqmighan döngi qalmas, dëdek munchaq assa kirmigen öyi qalmas.
Idiomatic meaning: set a beggar on horseback, and he'll ride to the devil; put a beggar on horseback and he'll ride it to death.

Goat has a beard, too.
> *Öchkidimu saqal bar.*
> **Idiomatic meaning:** A beard is not a sign of wisdom.

As I have God, I have no worries.
> *Xudayim bar ghemim yoq.*
> **Idiomatic meaning:** all things are possible with God.

God does nine, and I do thirty.
> *Xudayim qilar toqquz, men qilarmen ottuz.*
> **Idiomatic meaning:** man proposes, God disposes.

God forbid giving horns to a bad-tempered ox.
> *Üskek uygha tengri münggüz bermes.*

God has tomorrow.
> *Xudayimning etisi bar,.*
> **Idiomatic meaning:** tomorrow is another day.

Gold doesn't get rusted.
> *Altun chirimas.*
> **Idiomatic meaning:** if gold rusts what can iron do.

A good character is half a fortune.
> *Yaxshi xulq yërim dölet.*
> **Idiomatic meaning:** better a good cow than a cow of a good kind.

A good horse needs a whip, but a lousy horse needs a thousand.
> *Yaxshi atqa bir qamcha, yaman atqa ming qamcha.*
> **Idiomatic meaning:** a word to the wise is enough.

A good horse needs no whip.
> *Yaxshi atqa qamcha ketmes.*
> **Idiomatic meaning:** good wine needs no bush.

A good man is known for the job he does.
> *Yaxshi adem ishidin melum.*

A good man's bones rot, but his name endures.
Yaxshi ademning söngiki chirisimu, nami qalidu.

A good speech deserves the salute.
Yaxshi söz qedehke ige qilur.

A good visitor will come when the good food is served.
Yaxshi mëhman ash üstige këlidu.

The good wife is the blessing of the house.
Yaxshi xotun – öy berikiti.

A good wife is the foundation of the family.
Yaxshi xotun – öyge qozuq.

A good wife is the light of the house, and a good child is the ornament of the house.
Yaxshi xotun öyning chirighi, yaxshi bala öyning zinniti.
Idiomatic meaning: the grey mare is the better horse.

A good wife makes a good husband.
Erni er qilghanmu xotun, erni yer qilghanmu xotun.
Idiomatic meaning: two things prolong your life: a quiet heart and a loving wife.

A good wife makes a man a gentleman; a poor wife spoils even the best.
Yaxshi xotun erni er qilar yaman, yaman xotun yaxshi erni yer qilar.

A good word splits a stone, and a bad word breaks one's head.
Yaxshi gep tashni yarar, yaman gep bashni.
Idiomatic meaning: honey catches more flies than vinegar.

Goodness begets goodness.
Yaxshiliqqa yaxshiliq.
Idiomatic meaning: one good turn deserves another.

Goodness shall not perish.
Yaxshiliq yerde qalmas.
Idiomatic meaning: kindness, like a boomerang, always returns.

Goods flock together by their kind, people by their kind.
Mal türi bilen, adem xili bilen.
Idiomatic meaning: birds of a feather flock together.

A greedy man lost a bite of the charity food.
Nepsi yaman yette nezirdin quruq qaptu.
Idiomatic meaning: a bleating sheep loses a bite.

Grief consumes life.
Ghem ömürni yeydu.
Idiomatic meaning: fretting cares make grey hairs.

It does not grow unless you plant It and cannot be discovered until you try.
Tikmigüche ünmes, tilimigüche tëpilmas.

The habIt entered with the first feeding and departed with life's leaving.
Süt bilen kirgen xuy jan bilen chiqar.
Idiomatic meaning: what's bred in the bone will come out in the flesh.

Half of a month shines bright, while the other half resides in darkness.
Ayning onbeshi ayding, onbeshi qarangghu.

A hand given is better than a hand received.
Bergen qol, alghan qoldin yaxshi.
Idiomatic meaning: it is better to give than to receive.

A hand toying with a knife invites its own wound.
Pichaq bilen oynashma, qol këser.
Idiomatic meaning: do not play with edged tools.

There is no happiness without hardship and no pleasure without harmony.
Japa tartmay halawet yoq, inaq ötmey sa'adet (yoq)
Idiomatic meaning: no pain, no gain; nothing ventured, nothing gain.   .

The harvest of a flaxseed is recognised by its stalk.
Tëriqning bolushi kökidin melum.

Harvesting is not the job of a finch.
Xaman tepmek sündükning ishi emes.

Haste stumbles.
Aldirighan putlishar.
Idiomatic meaning: nothing should be done in haste but gripping a flea.

The hasty man's work remains undone.
Aldirighanning ishi chala.
Idiomatic meaning: nothing should be done in haste but gripping a flea.

A hasty person often finds themselves stuck along the road.
Aldirighan yolda qalar.
Idiomatic meaning: hasty climbers have sudden falls.

The hat shop is where the fate of baldness finds its remedy.
Tazning kelidighan yëri bökchining dukini.

Having been raised with respect, he mounted on the back of the one who nurtured him.
köterse geden'ge miniptu.
Idiomatic meaning: familiarity breeds contempt.

Having money allows you to enjoy a delicious soup even in the jungle.
pul bolsa janggalda shorpa.
Idiomatic meaning: money makes the mare to go.

He cuts himself with his own axe.
öz putigha özi palta chëpiptu.
Idiomatic meaning: Beaten with his owne rod.

He gave the dog bread, and It bIt his hand.
Itqa nan berse qolini chishleptu.
Idiomatic meaning: take an old dirty, hungry, mangy, sick and wet dog and feed him and wash him and nurse him back to health, and he will never turn on you and bite you. This is how man and dog differ.

He lost the watermelon to flaxseed.
Tëriqni dep tawuzdin ayrilip qaptu.
Idiomatic meaning: don't cut off your nose to spite your face.

He who can master self-control possesses the capacity to govern a city.
Özini sorighan sheher soraptu.
Idiomatic meaning: self trust is the first secret of success.

He who digs a hole for others finds himself falling into it.
Özi kolighan origha özi chüshüptu.
Idiomatic meaning: as you make your bed, so you must lie on it.

He who is afraid of dogs cannot be a beggar.
Ittin qorqqan abdal bolmaptu.
Idiomatic meaning: if you can't take the heat, get out of the kitchen.

He who is called a man at thirty shall be hailed as a lion by forty.
Ottuz yëshida er atalghan, qiriq yëshida shir atilar.
Idiomatic meaning: life begins at forty.

He who spits at the sky shall find It falling upon his face.
kökke tükürse yüzige chüsher.

He who steals a camel is a thief, and he who steals a button is still a thief.
Töge oghrilighanmu oghri, tügme oghrilighanmu oghri.
Idiomatic meaning: it's a sin to steal a pin.

The heads of two sheep cannot fIt within a single pot.
Ikki qoshqarning bëshi bir qazanda pishmas.

Health is a great wealth.
Ten saqliq - zor bayliq.
Idiomatic meaning: health is wealth.

A helpful stone never feels heavy.
Këreklik tashning ëghiri yoq.
Idiomatic meaning: keep a thing seven years and you'll always find a use for it.

The hen dreams of muck, while the goat dreams of the jungle.
Toxu danggal chüsheptu, öchke janggal (chüsheptu)
Idiomatic meaning: he that drinks beer, thinks beer.

The hero is tested within the team; the wise man is tested within the counsel.
Alp septe sinilar, dana yighinda.

Hold your spIt before foes, even with blood in your mouth.
Aghzinggha qan bolsimu, düshminingning aldida tükürme.

A horse roams and finds its stable, while a sheep circles the sheepfold.
At aylinip oqurni tapar, qoy aylinip qotanni (tapar)

Horses herd cannot be without a guide.
Qulan padisi yol bashlighuchisiz bolmas.

**A house with children resembles a bustling market, while
a house without children resembles a quiet graveyard.**
baliliq öy bazar; balisiz öy mazar.

A human child is not flawless.
Adem balisi eyipsiz bolmas.
Idiomatic meaning: to err is human, to forgive divine.

**Human children may pass away, yet their noble name
endures for eternity.**
Adem balisi yoqilar, yaxshi ëti menggülük qalar.
Idiomatic meaning: a good name is better than riches; a
man is not dead while his name is still spoken.

**The hungry do not choose when to eat, and the full do not
choose when to speak.**
Ach nëme yëmes, toq nëme dëmes.
Idiomatic meaning: out of the fullness of the heart the
mouth speaks.

A hungry man is an angry man.
Qorsiqi achning achchiqi yaman.
Idiomatic meaning: a hungry man is an angry man.

**I speak to my daughter, trusting my daughter-in-law will
listen.**
Qizim sanga eytay, kelinim sen angla.

I do thirty, God does nine.
Men qilarmen ottuz, xudayim qilar toqquz.
Idiomatic meaning: every man for himself, and God for
us all.

I may lack the attire, but my name is Baroness.
Qongamda ishtan yoq ëtim marjan büwi.

Ice drips water.
Muzdin su tamar.

Idlers tomorrow never comes.
Ërinchekning etisi tügimes.

If a sword remains in its sheath, It will gather rust.
Qilich qënida tursa dat basidu.
Idiomatic meaning: use it or lose it.

If an unlucky man enters the well, the wind will blow him out.
Biteley quduqqa kirse, shamal ëlip chiqar.

Even the sand will follow if an unlucky person falls into a well.
Bextsiz quduqqa chüshse, qum yaghar.

If It is God's will for a man to possess, he shall deliver It to his door.
Alla dëgen bendisige, ekilip bërer mehellisige.
Idiomatic meaning: if God had wanted man to fly, he would have given him wings.

If one dervish has a headache, It does not imply that all dervishes do.
Bir derwishning bëshi aghrisa, hemme derwishning bëshi aghrimas.

If one disregards the enemy, they risk losing their head.
Düshmenni sel chaghlisa, bashqa chiqar.

If one doesn't smile, they won't be approached.
Hinggaymisa dinggaymaydu.
Idiomatic meaning: there is always one who kisses, and one who turns the cheek.

If one honours the great, one will be blessed.
Ulughni ulughlisa qut bolur.

If the eye does not see, the heart does not love.
Köz körmise, köngül söymeydu.

Idiomatic meaning: what the eye doesn't see, the heart doesn't grieve over.

If the musk is removed from the bag, its fragrance permeates the air.
Iparliq xaltidin ipar ketse, hidi qalar.

If the pants are fine, you can sIt anywhere with ease.
Ishtini pütün xalighan yërige olturar.

If the private[15] knows the password, he shall not perish.
Im bilse, er ölmes.

If you are alive, you will witness many wonders.
Jan ësen bolsa, tangqalarliq ishlarni köp körer.

If you are humble, you will rise, if you are proud, you will sink.
Kemter bolsang ösersen, meghrurlansang chökersen.
Idiomatic meaning: pride comes before a fall.

If you befriend a good one, your flowers will bloom. If you befriend evil, your heart will be broken.
Yaxshi bilen dost bolsang, ëchilar chëchekliring. Yaman bilen dost bolsang yërilar yürekliring.
Idiomatic meaning: a man is known by the company he keeps.

If you buy a horse, seek advice for a month; if you marry, seek advice for a year.
At alsang ay këngesh, xotun alsang yil (këngesh)
Idiomatic meaning: never choose your women or your linen by candlelight.

If you cannot chew a stone, you must kiss It instead.
Tashni chaynighili bolmisa, söyüsh kërek.

---

[15] a private soldier is the lowest ranked soldier.

**If you follow the good, you will feast on meat; if you
follow the bad, you will receive a fist.**
*Yaxshigha egeshseng gösh yeysen, yaman'gha egeshseng
mush (yeysen)*
Idiomatic meaning: when the blind lead the blind, both
shall fall into a ditch.

If you cut wood, cut It long; if you cut iron, cut It short.
Yaghach kesseng uzun kes, tömür ketseng qisqa.

**If you do not eat, you starve; if you do not learn, you fall
behind.**
Yëmiseng ach qalisen, ögenmiseng këyin qalisen.

If you go to the city of cyclopes, close your one eye.
Yekcheshmining shehirige barsang bir közüngni qisiwal.
Idiomatic meaning: when in rome, do as the romans do.

If you go to the land of the blind, close one eye.
Qarighuning yurtigha barsang bir közüngni qisiwal.
Idiomatic meaning: when in rome, do as the romans do.

**If you marry, trouble may find you; if you don't, you may
wander as a homeless soul.**
Öy tutsang balada qalding, tutmisang talada (qalding)
Idiomatic meaning: needles and pins, needles and pins,
when a man marries, his trouble begins.

If you slaughter, even the sheep will tremble.
Boghuzlaymen dëseng, qoymu tipirlaydu .
idiomatic meaning: tread on a worm and it will turn.

If you sow one day early, you will reap ten days ahead.
Bir kün baldur tërisang, on kün baldur yighisen.
Idiomatic meaning: the sooner begun, the sooner done.

If you travel alone, your journey may be difficult.
Bolsang yalghuz seperlik, bolur ishing xeterlik.
Idiomatic meaning: he travels dangerously who travels
alone.

If your friend is a crow, you feast on filth.
Dostung qagha bolsa yëyishing poq.
Idiomatic meaning: if you lie down with dogs, you will get up with fleas; a man is known by the company he keeps,.

Ignorance is worse than poverty.
Bilimsizlik namratliqtin yaman.
Idiomatic meaning: ignorance is worse than poverty.

Ill An illiterate mullah speaks loudly; a crooked rolling pin makes noise.
Chala molla[16] walaqlaydu, egiri noghuch taraqlaydu.
Idiomatic meaning: a little knowledge is a dangerous thing; empty vessels make the most sound; it's the empty can that makes the most noise.

Imitators have a crooked mouth.
Doramchining aghzi puchuq.
Idiomatic meaning: imitation is the sincerest form of flattery.

In his haste, his pants tangled twice.
Aldirighanda ishtanbagh ikki chigilip qaptu.
Idiomatic meaning: more haste, less speed ; nothing should be done in haste but gripping a flea.

In the blind's world, day and night share no sight.
Qarighugha këche - kündüzning perqi yoq.
Idiomatic meaning: a blind man's wife needs no paint.

In the realm of virtue, language takes the lead.
Erdem bashi til.

---

[16] Mullah

The ingrained habIt endures until death.
> *Ögen'gen xuy ölgiche.*
> **Idiomatic meaning:** old habits die hard.

The investment of love is passion.
> *Muhebbetning desmayisi muhebbet.*
> **Idiomatic meaning:** love begets love.

It is an ill wolf that howls at its own den.
> *Böre uwisigha qarap huwlisa qotur bolur.*
> **Idiomatic meaning:** it's an ill bird that fouls its own nest.

It is better be beaten in a wide place than eat in a cramped place. (better deserted than crowded.)
> *Tar yerde ash yëgüche, keng yerde musht ye.*

Living a day like a tiger is better than living a thousand years like a rabbit.
> *Toshqandek ming yil yashighuche, yolwastek bir kün yasha.*
> **Idiomatic meaning:** better to live one day as a tiger than a thousand years as a sheep.

It is easier to destroy than to build.
> *Buzmaq asan, qurmaq tes.*
> **Idiomatic meaning:** glass, china, and reputation, are easily crack'd and never well mended.

It is haram[17] if It does not resemble its master.
> *Mal igisini dorimisa haram.*
> **Idiomatic meaning:** like father, like son; like mother, like daughter.

It is not the blind who lack sight but the blind who lack knowledge of letters.
> *közi körmigen qarighu emes, xet tonumighan qarighu.*

---

[17] Haram is an Arabic term meaning 'Forbidden'

Idiomatic meaning: there's none so blind as those who will not see.

It is preferable to endure solitude than to seek empathy from the ignorant.
Bilimsizge hal ëytquche ichingde sësitiwet.

It is better to have a wise enemy than an unwise friend.
Nadan dosttin zërek düshmen yaxshi.
Idiomatic meaning: better the devil you know (than the devil you don't)

It is the mark of a second fool to boast of oneself.
Özini maxtighan ikkinchi axmaq.
Idiomatic meaning: self-praise is no recommendation.

It takes a thousand years for a gecko to become a komodo dragon.
Patmichuqning kële bolmiqi ming yil.
Idiomatic meaning: it takes three generations to make a gentleman.

It went in one ear and out the other.
Bir qulaqtin kirip bir qulaqtin chiqiptu.
Idiomatic meaning: in one ear and out the other.

It's better to blow fire than to blow ashes.
Kül püwligüche, chogh püwligen tüzük.

It's better to die standing up than to live kneeling.
Tëz püküp yashighuche, tik turup ölgen yaxshi.
Idiomatic meaning: better to die on your feet than live on your knees; it is better to die on one's feet than live on one's knees.

It's better to go to the mill yourself and to express your words yourself.
Tügminingge özüng barghining yaxshi, gëpingni özüng qilghining yaxshi.

Idiomatic meaning: if you would be well served, serve yourself.

Just as a horse cannot run without oats, a hero cannot fight without support.
Arpisiz at qir ashalmas, yademchisiz alp sepni yimirelmes.
Idiomatic meaning: an army marches on its stomach.

Just as a lamb needs bone marrow, a child requires knowledge to thrive.
Oghlaq yiliksiz, bala bilimsiz bolmas.
.

Just as an empty spoon can't satisfy the mouth's plea, an empty promise fails to appease attentive ears.
Quruq qoshuq ëghizgha yarimas, quruq söz qulaqqa.
.

Kashgar's winter is fleeting, but its spring is a chilly embrace.
Qeshqerning qish az, soghuqi etiyaz.
Idiomatic meaning: march comes in like a lion and goes out like a lamb.

Keep your negativity confined within.
Chawangni chitqa yayma.
Idiomatic meaning: don't wash your dirty linen in public.

A kind word can soften even the hardest stone.
Chirayliq söz tashni yumshitar.
Idiomatic meaning: discretion is the better part of valour.

The king's order is an imperative.
Padishahning emri wajip.
Idiomatic meaning: the king can do no wrong.

Know thyself, and leave others be.
Özüngni bil, özgini qoy.

Idiomatic meaning: know thyself; paddle your own canoe; to each, his own.

Knowledge brings happiness.
Qutadghu bilik.

Knowledge is a sign of happiness.
Qut belgüsi bilik.

Knowledge is power.
Bilim küch.
Idiomatic meaning: knowledge is power.

Knowledge is the light of the mind.
Bilim eqilning chirighi.

A knowledgeable man is a pleasant man.
Bilimlik adem - yëqimliq adem.

A knowledgeable mind conquers a thousand with wisdom, whereas a strong hand defeats only one with strength.
Bilimi küchlük mingni yënger, biliki küchlük birni.

A knowledgeable person becomes a scholar; an ignorant person becomes a tyrant.
Bilimlik adem alim, bilimsiz adem zalim.

The land will remain, but customs may change.
Yurt qalar, törü qalmas.

The larger the camel, the greater the wound.
Töge qanche bolsa yëghiri shunche.
Idiomatic meaning: the bigger they are, the harder they fall; big fleas have little fleas upon their backs to bite them, and little fleas have lesser fleas, and so ad infinitum.

Lazy donkey's dung is heavy.
Yatqan ëshekning poqi torluq.
Idiomatic meaning: much cry and little wool.

The lazy man always has plenty of tomorrows.
Horunning etisi tola.

Learn in your youth, reap in your old age.
Yashliqingda bilim al, qërighanda ishqa sal.

Learn manners from the ill-mannered.
Edebni edepsizdin ögen.

Learning is akin to drilling a hole with a needle.
Bilim ëlish yingnide quduq kolighandek.

Let It be little, but the best.
Az bolsun, saz bolsun.

Let the past find its rest.
Ötken ishqa saliwat.
Idiomatic meaning: let bygones be bygones.

A liar never flourishes; a thief never gets rich.
Yalghanchi yaljimas, oghri bëyimas.
Idiomatic meaning: cheats never prosper; ill gotten goods never thrive.

Liar's promise is endless.
Yalghanchining wedisi (tügimes)

Life finds its essence in action.
Hayatliq - herikette.

Life has its limits, while knowledge knows no bounds.
Hayat cheklik, bilim cheksiz.
Idiomatic meaning: art is long and life is short.

Life is short.
Hayat qisqa.
Idiomatic meaning: life is too short.

Like a thread of tasbih[18], every problem possesses a
solution.
Teswining yipi bolidu, her ishning ëpi (bolidu)
Idiomatic meaning: every bullet has its billet.

To live a day, one must learn for a thousand days.
bir kün yashash üchün, ming kün ögen.
Idiomatic meaning: live and learn.

The bear devours the lone one; the separated one falls to
the wolf.
*Ayrilghanni ëyiq yeptu, bölün'genni böre (yeptu)/
ayrilghanni ëyiq yer, bölün'genni böri (yer)*
Idiomatic meaning: a house divided cannot stand.

Lonely widowhood is preferable to the company of a man
with an evil tongue.
Tili yaman erdin, yalghuz tulluq yaxshi.

Long-lasting illness has an immortal life.
Ölmes aghriq chiqmas jan.
Idiomatic meaning: a creaking door hangs longest.

He lost the meal in his hand to lick the crumbs on his
collar.
Yaqisidin yalaymen dep, ilikidikidin ayriliptu.

Luck doubles its favour upon the lucky.
Teleylikke qosh këler.

Make a trough for an unborn calf.
Tughulmighan mozaygha oqur saptu.
Idiomatic meaning: don't make clothes for a not yet born
baby.

---

[18] Prayer Beads

As a bird soars with its wings, a man finds strength alongside his horse.
Qush qaniti bilen, er ëti bilen.

The man lying in bed eats bread, while the worker nourishes on oleaster.
Ongda yatqan girde yeptu, ketmen chapqan jigde (yeptu)

Man pollutes the water, while water purifies the man.
Adem suni meynet qilar, su ademni pakiz (qilar)

The man who has consumed another's food becomes filled with modesty.
Ëghiz yëse, köz uyilar.

A man without knowledge is like a barren tree bearing no fruit.
Bilimsiz adem - mëwisiz derex.

A man without virtue loses the company of happiness.
Erdemsizdin qut këtidu.

Man's determination turns mountains into sand.
Erning gheyriti, taghni qum qilar.
Idiomatic meaning: faith will move mountains.

A man can't live forever; once in the grave, he never returns.
kishi menggü yashimas, görge kirse arqigha yanmas.

Man's words are one, and a saddle's thread is three.
Erning sözi bir, ëgerning köki üch.

Many people spoil the donkey.
Adem köp yerde ishek haram boptu.
Idiomatic meaning: too many cooks spoil the broth; councils of war never fight.

Match the remedy to the ailment and the chimney to the stove.

Këselge qarap dora, kanggha qarap mora.
Idiomatic meaning: circumstances alter cases; cut your coat according to your cloth.

Marriage is luck.
Nikah - ghayib.
Idiomatic meaning: marriage is a lottery.

Match the suitable ladle to the right pot, tIt for tat.
Undaq qazan'gha mundaq chömüch,.
Idiomatic meaning: ask a silly question and you get a silly answer; the door swings both ways.   .

There is measure in all things; the old wall is its base.
Hemme ish yoli bilen, kona tammu uli bilen.
Idiomatic meaning: there is measure in all things.

Measure seven times and cut once.
Yette ölchep bir kes.
Idiomatic meaning: look before you leap,measure seven times, cut once; measure twice, cut once; think twice, cut once.

There is no death for a messenger.
Elchige ölüm yoq.
Idiomatic meaning: don't shoot the messenger.

The might of the pen triumphs over the might of the sword.
Qilichning küchidin, qelemning küchi artuq.
Idiomatic meaning: the pen is mightier than the sword.

A mill built on unfavourable ground is destined to drown in flood.
Nabab yerge tügmen qursa, kütmigende yar këter.

Misfortunes never come noticed.
Bala qaza körünüp kelmes, put - qolini sanggilitip.
Idiomatic meaning: misfortunes never come on their own.

Modesty and morality are sisters.
Haya bilen exlaq, acha bilen singil.

Money has no language.
pulning tili yoq.

Money makes money.
Pulni pul tapidu.
Idiomatic meaning: money makes money.

The monkey claims the throne's height when the mountain lacks a tiger's might.
Taghda yolwas bolmisa, maymun padishah bolur.
Idiomatic meaning: when the cat's away, the mice will play.

Morality cannot be purchased in the market, and the immoral find themselves isolated.
Edeb - exlaq bazarda sëtilmas, edebsizge hëch kishi qëtilmas.

The more cunning the hunter becomes, the cleverer the bear adapts.
Owchi qanche hile bilse, ëyiqmu shunche yol bilidu.

A mother nourishes ten children, yet ten children cannot care for a mother.
Bir ana on balini baqar, on bala bir anini baqalmas.

The mother of the disease is influenza.
Këselning anisi zukam.

The mother of songs is muqam.
Naxshining anisi muqam.

The mountain in sight is not far.
Körün'gen tagh yiraq emes.

Mountains stand apart, but man connects heart to heart.
Tagh taghqa qowushmas, adem ademge qowushur.

Moving home three times is as bad as losing a goat and its kid.
Üch qëtim öy köchseng , bir oghlaghliq öchkige ziyan.

The mullah always appears better in other people's villages.
Yandiki mollam, bar mollam, yiraqtiki mollam damollam.
Idiomatic meaning: the grass is always greener on the other side of the fence; a prophet is not recognized in his own land.

My bloody fist is better than a stranger's delicious bite.
Yatning yaghliq loqmisidin özining qanliq mushti yaxshi.

My smoky house, my warm house.
Isliq öyüm, issiq öyüm.
Idiomatic meaning: home is home, as the devil said when he found himself in the court of session.

A neglected stick may break the head.
Közge ilmighan chomaq qangsharni yarar.

A neighbour's possession seems twice as grand.
Qoshnamning qosh körüner.
Idiomatic meaning: the grass is always greener on the other side of the fence.

No matter how foolish, a companion is good; no matter how crooked, the road is good.
Herqanche exmeq bolsimu, hemrah yaxshi, herqanche egri bolsimu, yol yaxshi.
Opposite in english: better to be alone than in bad company.

No matter how old the jacket is, it's still good for rain.
Chapan qanche kona bolsimu yamghurgha yarar.

No matter how sharp the knife is, It cannot carve its own handle.
Pichaq qanche ittik bolsimu, öz sëpini yonuyalmas.

Nonsense weighs heavy, burdening even the humblest donkey.
Quruq gep ishekke yük.

Bilmeslik eyib emes, sorimasliq eyib.
Bilmeslik eyib emes, sorimasliq eyib.
Idiomatic meaning: the only stupid question is the one that is not asked.

Oily gourd ladles are always oily gourd ladles.
Yaghliq qapaq haman yaghliq qapaq.
Idiomatic meaning: once a priest, always a priest; once a whore, always a whore;.

The old bird cannot be fooled by the miller's bran.
Qëri qushqach këpekke aldanmas.
Idiomatic meaning: you cannot catch old birds with chaff.

The old ox fears not the axe's presence.
Qëri öküz paltidin qorqmas.

Old quiver provides a strong arrow.
Uprighan ya qëpidin, mezmut ya chiqidu.

Oleaster cannot be almond, wise cannot be irrational.
Jigdidin badam chiqmas, bilimlik kishidin nadan (chiqmas)
Idiomatic meaning: you can't make a silk purse out of a sow's ear.

Omentum is not a substitute for cooking oil.
Chawa yagh su yëghining ornini basalmas.

The one once burnt by milk, blows on yoghurt to cool.
Süt ichip aghzi köygen qëtiqnimu püwlep icher.
Idiomatic meaning: a burnt child dreads the fire; once burnt, twice shy.

The one destined to be an ox is apparent even in its calfhood.
Öküz bolidighan kala, mozay chëghidila belgülik bolidu.

The one who sipped the yogurt escaped, while the one who licked It faced capture.
Qëtiq ichken qutuldi, ayaq yalighan tutuldi.
Idiomatic meaning: little thieves are hanged, but great ones escape.

On the first day, he's a guest; on the second, a visitor. By the third day, he's a burden; by the fourth, a stick is needed to drive him away.
Birinchi küni mëhman, ikkinchi küni xiyman. Üchinchi küni mayaq, tötinchi küni tayaq.
Idiomatic meaning: fish and guests stink after three days.

Once a shot is fired and words are spoken, they cannot be withdrawn.
Atqan oqni yandurghili bolmas, chiqqan sözni qayturghili (bolmas)
Idiomatic meaning: what's done cannot be undone; a word spoken is past recalling.

Once life has departed, the recitation of yasin[19] holds no significance.
Ölgendin këyin 'yasin' oqughanning nëme paydisi.
Idiomatic meaning: it is no use crying over spilt milk; it is too late to shut the stable-door after the horse has bolted; when a thing is done advice comes too late.

Once spoken, words cannot be undone.
Chiqqan sözni qayturghili (bolmas)
Idiomatic meaning: what's done cannot be undone.

---

[19] One of the Quranic Surahs

Once your time has passed, so too has your happiness.
Waqting ketti - bexting ketti.

One crow does not make a winter.
Bir qagha bilen qish kelmes.

One false stitch unravels forty threads.
Qildin ketseng qiriqtin këtisen.
Idiomatic meaning: a miss is as good as a mile.

One flower does not make a spring.
Bir gül bilen bahar bolmas.
Idiomatic meaning: one swallow does not make a
summer.

**One hand washes the other, and together they wash the
face.**
Qol qolini yusa, qol yüzni yuyar.
Idiomatic meaning: one hand washes the other; you
scratch my back, i'll scratch yours; if every man would
sweep his own doorstep the city would soon be clean.

One locks the door after It has been robbed.
Öyni oghri alghandin këyin ishik taqaptu.
Idiomatic meaning: it is too late to shut the stable door
after the horse has bolted.

One person has one mind; many people have many minds.
Birning eqli bir bolidu, köpning eqli köp (bolidu)
Idiomatic meaning: when spider webs unite, they can tie
up a lion; Many hands make light work.

One rotten pear can spoil a thousand.
Bir sësiq amut mingni buzar.
Idiomatic meaning: the rotten apple injures its
neighbour; one rotten apple will spoil the whole barrel;
one scabbed sheep mars the whole flock.

**One seeks a shroud from the departed and searches for a
cattail in the desert.**

ölüktin këpen tileptu, qumluqtin yiken (tileptu)
Idiomatic meaning: what can you expect from a pig but
a grunt?.

**One who cannot shoot blames the bullet, and one who
cannot defecate blames the faeces.**
Atalmas oqidin, chichalmas poqidin körer.
Idiomatic meaning: a bad workman blames his tools.

One who fears the birds cannot sow the flaxseed.
Qushqachtin qorqqan tëriq tërimaptu.
Idiomatic meaning: if you don't like the heat, get out of
the kitchen.

One who fears the wolf can tend to the sheep.
Böridin qorqqan qoy baqmas.
Idiomatic meaning: if you can't stand the heat, get out of
the kitchen.

One who is not present has no face.
Özi yoqning yüzi yoq.
Idiomatic meaning: he who is absent is always in the
wrong.

**One who receives free food complains about the absence
of salt.**
Bikargha tamaq berse, tuzi kem deptu.
Idiomatic meaning: don't look a gift horse in the mouth.

One will not breastfeed the baby unless It cries.
Yighlimisa emchek salmaydu.
Idiomatic meaning: don't mend what ain't broken; if it
ain't broke, don't fix it.

Out of sight, out of mind.
Közdin yiraq, köngüldin yiraq.
Idiomatic meaning: out of sight, out of mind.

The paint is not to blame for the effects of ageing caused by the passage of time.
Zaman qëritqan'gha boyaq eyib emes.

Patience is gold.
Sewrning tëgi altun.
Idiomatic meaning: patience is a virtue.

Patience is required with the green apricot, or It shall pass undigested as a whole.
Aldirap ghora yëmeng, pütün chiqar.
Idiomatic meaning: nothing should be done in haste but gripping a flea.

Patience paves the path to one's goal.
Sewri qilghan muradigha yëter.
Idiomatic meaning: he that can have patience can have what he will; all things come to those who wait; good things come to those who wait.

People are known through words, while animals recognise through scent.
Kishi sözliship, haywan hidliship.

People's word is God's word.
Elning sözi xudaning sözi.
Idiomatic meaning: the voice of the people is the voice of God.

A perforated bead won't be left in vain.
töshük marjan yerde qalmas.

Pillow supports hunger.
Achliqni yastuq kötürer.

Polite mouth pours out beautiful words.
Edeblik ëghizning sözi güzel.
Idiomatic meaning: handsome is as handsome does; pretty is as pretty does.

He who raises the smoke shall bear the burn.
Kim tütün qopursa, özi islinur.

A rat born in a mill is not afraid of thunders.
*Tügmende tughulghan chashqan, hawaning
güldürliginidin qorqmas.*

Regret diminishes sin; charity lessens misfortune.
Töwe gunahni yer, sediqe balani.
Idiomatic meaning: charity covers a multitude of sins;
confession is good for the soul.

To remove the eye's dirt, one makes a man blind.
Chapiqini alimen dep qarighu qiptu.
Idiomatic meaning: when you are in a hole, stop digging.

Respect the learned.
Bilimlikke hörmet qil.

**A right word can splIt a stone, but a crooked word can
break a head.**
Toghra söz tashni yarar, egri söz bashni (yarar)
Idiomatic meaning: honey catches more flies than
vinegar; a soft answer turneth away wrath.

A right word is sharper than a sword.
Toghra söz qilichtin ötkür.
Idiomatic meaning: the pen is mightier than the sword.

**Rising early brings grace, while waking late leads to a
clumsy pace.**
Seher qopqan sa'adet, waqche qopqan palaket.
Idiomatic meaning: the early bird catches the worm;
early to bed and early to rise, makes a man healthy,
wealthy, and wise.

A rope breaks at its weak link.
Arghamcha ajiz yëridin üzülidu.
Idiomatic meaning: a chain is no stronger than its
weakest link.

People's satisfaction is God's satisfaction.
El razi xuda razi.

**To savour the fruit's sweetness, tend to the roots with
care.**
Derextin mëwe alay dëseng yiltizini asra.

**People will search even within their mother's embrace
when something is lost.**
Nerse yoqatqan kishi, anisining qoyninimu axturidu.

The seeds you sow determine the fruits you reap.
Nëme tërisang shuni alisan.
Idiomatic meaning: garbage in, garbage out; as you sow,
so you reap; as you bake, so shall you brew; as you brew,
so shall you bake; he who plants thorns should not expect
to gather roses.

Seeing once is superior to hearing a thousand times.
Ming anglighandin bir körgen ela.
Idiomatic meaning: seeing is believing.

Seek guidance from the caravan.
Yolni karwandin sora.
Idiomatic meaning: to know the road ahead ask those
coming back.

To seek wisdom, you must embrace learning.
Eqil tapay dëseng ögen.

**Seek virtue and pursue knowledge humbly; pride without
integrity crumbles in adversity.**
*Pezilet tile, öginish bilen meghrurlanma, peziletsiz turup
meghrurlansa, sinaqta hoduqidu.*

Servant of the four walls.
Töt tamning quli.
Idiomatic meaning: i'm stuck between the four walls of
burdens.

The share of a liar is less, its life is short.
  Yalghanchining risqi qisqa, ömri kötey.
  Idiomatic meaning: cheats never prosper.

A shot will not return, the past cannot be called back.
  Atqan oq yënip kelmes, ötken waqit qaytip (kelmes)
  Idiomatic meaning: things past cannot be recalled.

A sign is enough to the wise.
  Eqilge isharet nadangha juwalduruz.

Silence is better than telling a lie.
  Yalghanchi bolghuche gacha bol.

A silk patch befits silk fabric, while a wool patch suits woollen material.
  Yipeklik yamaq yipek rextke, yung yamaq yung rextke layiq këlidu.

A single goose does not make a sound.
  Yalghuz ghazning awazi chiqmas.

A single hand cannot clap.
  Yekke qoldin chawak chiqmas.
  Idiomatic meaning: it takes two to make a quarrel; it takes two to tango.

The spirIt is will, but power is weak.
  Arman'gha chushluq derman yoq.
  Idiomatic meaning: the spirit is willing but the flesh is weak.

A slap is better than an empty promise.
  Quruq geptin kachat yaxshi.

A small act of honesty outweighs the weight of a colossal ill-repute.
  Qildek semimiyetlik, pildek ataqtin ela.
  Idiomatic meaning: he that has an ill name is half hanged; a hungry man is an angry man.

A sniper is known for his shot.
> *Mergen atqan oqdin biliner.*
> **Idiomatic meaning:** a carpenter is known by his chips.

A son takes after his father, and a daughter takes after her mother.
> *Oghul dadisini doraydu, qiz anisini (doraydu)*
> **Idiomatic meaning:** like father, like son; like mother, like daughter.

Soul for soul, blood for blood.
> *Jan'gha jan, qan'gha qan.*
> **Idiomatic meaning:** an eye for an eye and a tooth for a tooth.

A sound mind in a sound body.
> *Saghlam tende saghlam eqil.*
> **Idiomatic meaning:** sound mind, sound body.

Sow diligence in youth to reap happiness in adulthood.
> *Kichikide qattiq tirishsa, chong bolghanda söyüner.*

A spoiled child is good for nothing.
> *Erke ösken bala, bolidu ishqa chala.*

Stab yourself with a knife first; if It does not hurt, then stab others.
> *Pichaqni özüngge sal, aghrimisa kishige (sal)*
> **Idiomatic meaning:** do as you would be done by. Do unto others as you would they should do unto you.

Stand your ground; fear not the king.
> *yoldin chiqma, xandin qorma.*
> **idiomatic meaning:** do right and fear no man.

A stone is valued most in its own home.
> *Tashmu chüshken yerde ëziz.*

A stranger's loyalty ends with the meal; a relative's lasts a lifetime.

Yat yëgiche, tughqan ölgiche.
Idiomatic meaning: blood is thicker than water.

Strength lies in numbers.
Köpning küchi köp.
Idiomatic meaning: many hands make light work; when spider webs unite, they can tie up a lion.

Stretch your legs within the bounds of your coverlet.
Yotqan'gha bëqip put sun.
Idiomatic meaning: stretch your arms no further than your sleeve will reach; don't bite off more than you can chew.

Strike while the iron is hot.
Tömürni qiziqida soq.
Idiomatic meaning: make hay while the sun shines; strike while the iron is hot.

Study cultivates wisdom within the mind.
Köp izdenseng eqil taparsen.

Sweet words coax the snake from its nest, while bitter words may turn even a Muslim atheist.
Shirin sözliseng, yilan indin chiqar, achchiq sözliseng musulman dindin (chiqar)
Idiomatic meaning: with a sweet tongue and kindness, you can drag an elephant by a hair.

A taker is the lion, and the giver is the mouse.
Ëlimchi arslan, bërimchi chashqan.

The tail of a liar is short.
Yalghanchining quyruqi bir tutam,.
Idiomatic meaning: cheats never prosper.

Talk about the man, and he is bound to appear.
Kimning gëpini qilsa shu keptu.
Idiomatic meaning: talk of the devil, and he is bound to appear; talk of the devil and he's sure to appear.

Teach while the child is young.
Balini yashtin öget.
Idiomatic meaning: bend the willow while it is young.

A teacher does not laugh; he cannot stop if he laughs.
Xelpet külmeydu, külse tëliqip qalidu.
Idiomatic meaning: it never rains but it pours.

Thanks for the giving.
Berginige shükür qil.
Idiomatic meaning: when all fruit fails, welcome haws.

Thick ice doesn't freeze overnight.
Qëlin muz bir künde muzlimaydu.
Idiomatic meaning: rome was not built in a day.

A thief's heart quickens its pace.
Oghrining yüriki pok - pok.
Idiomatic meaning: a guilty conscience needs no accuser; there's no peace for the wicked.

Thieves are doubters.
Oghri gumanxor.
Idiomatic meaning: evil doers are evil dreaders.

Think first, then speak.
Awwal oyla, andin sözle.
Idiomatic meaning: think first and speak afterwards; think before you speak.

This, too, shall pass.
Bumu ötüp këtidu.
Idiomatic meaning: this, too, shall pass.

Thorn in the foot reveals the truth to the barefoot traveller.
Oghri tiken yayaqqa heqiqetni chüshendüridu.

Those adorned with jade need not fear the lightning's blade.

Kimning yënida qashtëshi bolsa, uninggha chaqmaq tegmeydu.

Though a cave It may be, my dwelling surpasses grandeur.
Öngkür bolsimu öyüm yaxshiken.
Idiomatic meaning: home is home though it's never so homely.

Though penniless, the cat's heart still longs for meat.
Müshükning bir puli yoq göshke amraq.
Idiomatic meaning: all cats love fish but hate to get their paws wet.

Though the camel is large, its dung is small.
Töge chong bolghini bilen, mayiqi chong emes.

Through collection, even grains of sand can amass into a mountain.
Yighsang qummu tagh bolidu.

Through patience, the green apricot ripens to sweet fruition.
Sewri qilsang ghoridin halwa pishar.
Idiomatic meaning: all things come to those who wait; good things come to those who wait.

Through the aid of fellow men, a man truly becomes.
Adem adem bilen adem bolar.
Idiomatic meaning: no man is an island.

There is thunder but no rain.
Güldüri bar, yamghuri yoq.
Idiomatic meaning: big thunder, little rain.

Time is impatient and does not waIt for any.
Waqt aldirangghu, saqlap turmaydu.
Idiomatic meaning: time and tide wait for none.

Time slips away unnoticed, and no one is eternal.
Zaman öter, kishi tuymas adem balisi menggü qalmas.

A timid heart is quick to fight.
Qorqqan awwal mush kötürer.
Idiomatic meaning: the weakest go to the wall.

Today's sheep lungs are better than tomorrow's sheep tail.
Etiki quyruqtin bügünki öpke yaxshi.
Idiomatic meaning: better an egg today than a hen tomorrow; a bird in the hand is worth two in the bush; fifty percent of something is better than one hundred percent of nothing.

Too many mullahs spoil the meat.
Molla köp bolsa qoy haram bolar.
Idiomatic meaning: too many cooks spoil the broth.

Too much sleep leads to hunger.
Köp uxlisang ach qalisen.

True love requires no counsellor.
Muhebbetke meslihetchining këriki yoq.
Idiomatic meaning: love will find a way.

Try three times; the third attempt brings luck.
Mertem mertem üch mertem.
Idiomatic meaning: third time lucky.

Two is better than one, and an oleaster is better than empty promises.
Birdin ikki yaxshi, quruq geptin jigde (yaxshi)
Idiomatic meaning: half a loaf is better than no bread; fifty percent of something is better than one hundred percent of nothing; something is better than nothing.

Two swords cannot fIt in one sheath.
Qosh qilich bir qin'gha sighmas.

An ugly man carries an ugly manner.
Özi setning qiliqi set.
Idiomatic meaning: handsome is as handsome does.

Unable to taste the meat, the cat declares no interest in others' fare.
Müshük qozuqtiki chawa yaghqa tëgelmey, kishining mëli manga yarashmas der.

Unity is strength.
Ittipaqliq küch.
Idiomatic meaning: unity is strength.

The universe possesses eyes and ears.
alemning köz - quliqi bar.
Idiomatic meaning: fields have eyes, and woods have ears.

Utilise your strength rather than diminishing yourself.
Özüngni xar qilghuche küchüngni xar qil.
Idiomatic meaning: better to light one's candle than to curse the darkness.

As violence enters, discipline and manners depart through the window.
Zorluq-zombuluq ishiktin kirse, insap we qaide-yosun tünglüktin chiqar.

The value of a tree lies in its fruit.
Tërek miwisi bilen qimmiet.

Virtue is the beautiful adornment of a person.
Exlaq adem zinniti.

Time is a shot.
Waqit atqan oq.
Idiomatic meaning: time flies.

Waste breeds devastation.
Israpchiliq - xarabliq.

Watch your words, as they may echo back to you.
nëme dëseng shuni anglaysen.

The water of the new clay pots is cold.
Yëngi küpning süyi soghuq.
Idiomatic meaning: new brooms sweep clean.

The water of the new lake is sweet.
Yëngi kölning süyi tatliq.
Idiomatic meaning: new brooms sweep clean.

When the garden lacks flowers, the nightingale's song fades away.
Bagda gül bolmisa, bulbul kelip sayramas.

There is no wealth more remarkable than knowledge.
Bilimdin artuq bayliq yoq.

The wealthy go to the market, while the poor go to the shrine.
Puli bar bazargha mangar, puli yoq mazargha (mangar)

What does my teacher do? Works intermittently.
Xelpet nëme ish qilidu? Tikip-söküp ish qilidu.
Idiomatic meaning: insanity is doing the same thing over and over, expecting different results.

What you do to others returns to yourself.
Her kim qilsa, özige qilar.
Idiomatic meaning: as you sow, so shall you reap; every herring must hang by its own gill.

What you hear is lies, what you see is the truth.
Qulaq bilen anglighan yalghan, köz bilen körgen rast.
Idiomatic meaning: believe nothing of what you hear, and only half of what you see.

What you pray for, you might get; if you sow, you shall reap.
Tiliseng taparsen, tërisang orarsen.

Idiomatic meaning: he that follows frets, frets will
follow him; be careful what you pray for, you might get it.

When a crow imitates a goose, It risks breaking its foot.
Qagha ghazni dorisa, puti sünar.

When a fox attacks its brother, It becomes rabid.
Tülke öz inige ürse, qotur bolar.

**When a lamb is born in a sheep's shed, verdant grass shall
line the stream.**
Ëghilda oghlaq tughulsa, ëriqta oti üner.

When a lion roars, a horse's hooves tremble in fear.
Arslan hörkirse, at ayighi kalwalishidu.

**When choosing a melon, the owner picks It with both
hands.**
Qoghun tallansa, igisimu ikki qoli bilen tallar.

**When disaster arrives, It often comes in pairs, each one
leading the other.**
Bala kelse qoshlap këler, bir - birini bashlap (këler)
Idiomatic meaning: bad things come in threes;
misfortunes never come singly.

When Grandma can't dance, she blames the dance floor.
Momay usul bilmes, yërim tar der.
Idiomatic meaning: a bad workman blames his tools,.

When in a hurry, the donkey chooses to lie down.
Aldirighanda ëshiki yëtiwaptu.

**When lightning strikes, It ignites; when words are
explained, the purpose is known.**
*Chaqmaq chüshse ot tutishar, söz anglitilsa meqset
biliner.*

When a man needs it, he drinks water from his boots.
Er bëshigha kün kelse, ötük bilen su këcher.
Idiomatic meaning: needs must when the devil drives.

When modesty departs, misfortune draws near.
Haya ketse bala këlur.

**When owner fades away, the goat bears the name
Abdulrahman.**
Öy igisi bolmisa, öchkining ëti abduraxman.
Idiomatic meaning: when the cat's away, the mice will
play.

When praised, his ego overflows like a running river.
Maxtap qoysa malxiyigha chiqiriptu.
Idiomatic meaning: the higher the monkey climbs the
more he shows his tail.

When the crows fight, the hunter will delight.
Ikki qagha poq talashsa, owchigha payda.
Idiomatic meaning: while two dogs are fighting for a
bone, a third runs away with it.

When the guest arrives, luck walks through the door.
mëhman kelse qut këler.
.

When the lion is old, guard the mouse's nest.
Arslan qërisa, chashqanning uwasini köziter.

**When the qadi is hungry, he goes to the bazaar; when the
sopi is hungry, he turns to the mazar. (graveyard)**
*Qazi ach qalsa bazar këzidu, sopi ach qalsa mazar
(këzidu)*

When the unlucky one steals, the full moon shows up.
Biteley oghriliqqa chiqsa ayding boptu.

**When there is a sign, you are not lost; with knowledge,
you are not lost for words.**
Belge bolsa yoldin azmas, bilim bolsa sözdin qaymas.

**When time refuses to conform to your desires, adjust to
its rhythm.**
Zaman sanga baqmisa, sen zaman'gha baq.
Idiomatic meaning: if the mountain will not come to
mahomet, mahomet must go to the mountain.

When you assign a task to a child, you must follow up.
Kichik balini ishqa buyrusang, arqisidin özüng bar.
Idiomatic meaning: never send a boy to do a man's job.

You must give when you take, and return when you go.
Almaqning bermiki bar, barmaqning kelmiki (bar)
Idiomatic meaning: give the devil his due; give and take
is fair play.

Where is the infallible sage?.
Xatalashmighan danishmen nede?.
Idiomatic meaning: if you don't make mistakes you
don't make anything.

Where many unite, mountains can be moved.
Köpning küchi tagh kötirer.
Idiomatic meaning: many hands make light work.

Where pride abounds, the fall awaits.
Meghrurlansang chökersen.
Idiomatic meaning: pride comes before the fall.

Where the busy one ventures, trails the one unhurried.
Aldirighan nede këtip baridu, aldirimighanning keynide.
Idiomatic meaning: more haste, less speed.

**Where the sheep meets its stake, the man confronts his
sins in full.**
Qoy özining pëyide ësilidu, adem öz gunahini tartidu.

Idiomatic meaning: every tub must stand on its own bottom.

Where the sun illuminates the dawn, books awaken the conscience.
Quyash tangni yorutar, kitab angni yorutar.

Where there are no fish, there shall be no cat.
Quruq gepke müshükmu aptapqa chiqmaydu.
Idiomatic meaning: nothing comes of nothing.

Where there is wisdom, there is greatness.
Eqil - idrak qeyerde bolsa, ulughluq shu yerde bolidu.
Idiomatic meaning: where bees are, there is honey.

While not dead, hope forever persists.
Chiqmighan janda ümid bar.
Idiomatic meaning: where there is a will, there is a way.

While the two horses fight, the donkey suffers.
Ikki at tëpisher, arida qalghan ëshek öler.

While two male camels fight, the gadfly dies.
Ikki bughra ekisher, arida köküyün yanjilar.

While two rams fight, the dog runs away with the bone.
Ikki qoshqar soqushsa itqa ozuq chiqar.
Idiomatic meaning: while two dogs are fighting for a bone, a third runs away with it.

Who knows the age of a crow, and who can unravel the wickedness within a man?.
Qaghining qërisini kim biler, kishining alisini kim tapar.

Whoever guards their mouth also saves their own life.
Ëghiz saqlighan janni saqlar.
Idiomatic meaning: a shut mouth catches no flies.

Whomever your brother weds, becomes your sister-in-law.
Akang kimni alsa yenggeng shu.

A wife is an angel of the home.
Xotun kishi öy perishtisi.

A wife is the flower of the house.
Xotun kishi öyning güli.
Idiomatic meaning: the grey mare is the better horse.

If the wind doesn't blow, the tree stays still.
Shamal chiqmisa derex lingshimas.
Idiomatic meaning: no smoke without fire; there is no smoke without fire.

To attain wisdom, you must invest in books.
Eqil tapay dёseng kitab al.

The wise blame themselves; the ignorant blame friends.
Bilimlik özini eyibler, bilimsiz dostini.

With a wife, your home becomes a garden; without one, your home resembles a desert.
Khotunung bar öyüng gül, khotunung yoq öyüng chöl.

The wind disperses black clouds, while bribe opens the doors of government.
Qara bulutni yel achar, hökümet ishikini para achar.

Winter is blind.
Qish közi qarighu.

Wisdom does not lie in age but in the mind.
Eqil yashta emes bashta.
Idiomatic meaning: Wisdom doesn't come with age.

A wise man has many measures.
Bilimlikning tedbiri köp.

**I wish there were only summer, no winter, only food, with
no need for work.**
Yaz bolsa, qish bolmisa, ash bolsa ish (bolmisa)
Idiomatic meaning: the cat would eat fish, but would not
wet her feet.

**With diligent preparation during ploughing, harvest
brings unity, not quarrelling.**
*Sapan waqtida puxtiliq bolsa, xaman waqtida jangjal
bolmas.*

**With each grain amassed, sand transforms into a
mountain.**
Qum yighilsa tagh bolur.
Idiomatic meaning: take care of the pence and the
pounds will take care of themselves.

With preparedness, disaster is averted.
Teyyar tursang apet körmeysen.
Idiomatic meaning: forewarned is forearmed.

Within the embrace of a wife, a house finds its essence.
Öyni öy etken xotun.

**Without knowledge, the head becomes a burden to the
body.**
Bilimsiz bash, gewdige yük.

Without sacrifice, beauty remains elusive.
Jandin kechmigiche janan'gha yetkili bolmas.
Idiomatic meaning: faint heart ne'er won fair lady.

**Without the eye of wisdom, the eye is but a hollow in the
wall.**
Eqilning közi bolmisa, köz dëgen tam tüshüki.

Without theft, the thief finds no solace in slumber.
Oghri oghriliqini qilmisa, közige uyqu kelmes.
Idiomatic meaning: a leopard never changes its spots.

Wolf does not devour its neighbours.
  Böre qoshnisini yëmes.
  Idiomatic meaning: hawks will not pick out hawks' eyes.

Words of the learned are clear.
  Bilimlikning gëpi roshen.
  Idiomatic meaning: who knows most, speaks least.

Work hard instead of boasting.
  Gepdan bolghuche ishchan bol.

Work is better on its time; the trader is at a profit.
  Ish peytide, sodiger paydida.

Work thrives in unity; power flourishes in togetherness.
  Ish ömlükte, küch birlikte.
  Idiomatic meaning: union is strength.

Work with counsel finds resolution; work without It faces struggle.
  Këngeshlik ish üzlishar, këngeshsiz ish buzular.
  Idiomatic meaning: trouble shared is trouble halved.

The worked bite, the unworked fades.
  Ishligen chishleydu, ishlimigen chishlimeydu.
  Idiomatic meaning: if you won't work you shan't eat.

Worms cling to a soft tree.
  Bosh yaghachni qurt yeydu.

The wound from a sword may heal, but a wound from the tongue cannot.
  Tigh yarisi këter, til yarisi ketmes.
  Idiomatic meaning: a blow with a word strikes deeper than a blow with a sword.

The wrath of the ignorant is a formidable force.
  Bilimi azning achchiqi yaman.